DEADLINES

DEADLINES

OBITS OF MEMORABLE BRITISH COLUMBIANS

Tom Hawthorn

HARBOUR PUBLISHING

Harbour Publishing Co. Ltd.
P.O. Box 219, Madeira Park, BC, V0N 2H0
www.harbourpublishing.com

Cover design by Anna Comfort O'Keeffe
Text design by Mary White
Printed and bound in Canada

Harbour Publishing acknowledges financial support from the
Government of Canada through the Canada Book Fund and the Canada
Council for the Arts, and from the Province of British Columbia through
the BC Arts Council and the Book Publishing Tax Credit.

 Canada Council   Conseil des Arts
for the Arts   du Canada
 BRITISH COLUMBIA
ARTS COUNCIL
An agency of the Province of British Columbia

Library and Archives Canada Cataloguing in Publication

Hawthorn, Tom
    Deadlines : obits of memorable British Columbians / Tom
Hawthorn.

ISBN 978-1-55017-581-3

    1. British Columbia—Biography. 2. Obituaries—British Columbia.
I. Title.

FC3805.H38 2012   920.0711   C2012-904298-6

CONTENTS

WRITERS

ATHLETES

CHARACTERS

PREFACE

In these pages you'll meet some fascinating people. They have two things in common—they all have a connection to British Columbia and they're all dead.

You'll meet an aviatrix and a Communist; a boxer named Baby Face and a wrestler called Mean Gene; a yodeling cowboy singer named Alberta Slim and the real-life model for James Bond.

Spoony Singh won and lost fortunes in the sawmill business in British Columbia before opening the Hollywood Wax Museum. Bergie Solberg lived a hermit's life in the bush on the Sechelt Peninsula, where she was known as the Cougar Lady. Doug Hepburn, born cross-eyed and with a club foot, became the world's strongest man.

Donald Hings was an inveterate tinkerer credited with inventing the walkie-talkie. Cecil Green was a poor schoolboy who went into electronics, making a fortune at Texas Instruments that he then proceeded to give away.

An obituary is a profile in which the subject cannot grant an interview, so we obituarists behave as newsroom jackals, rending bits of reportage and quotation from reporters who have come before. Perhaps it is for this reason the obituary desk is considered the lowest spot in the newsroom hierarchy. It is a job most typically assigned to cub reporters and burned-out veterans, recovering alcoholics and those who still seek inspiration in the bottom of a bottle. In his novel *The Imperfectionists*, Tom Rachmann describes the end product of an obituarist's workday: "decades of a person's life condensed into a few paragraphs, with a final resting place at the bottom of page nine, between Puzzle-Wuzzle and World Weather."

Luckily for me, most of these stories originally appeared in the *Globe and Mail*, for which I also write a human-interest column twice a week. The *Globe* dedicates a full page of every edition each publication day to obits, following a path blazed by the late Hugh Massingberd, the obituaries editor at *The Telegraph* in London. As his obit in that paper noted, he "had to reinvent the whole concept of the form, substituting for the grave and ceremonious tribute the sparkling celebration of life."

Writing an obituary is the most intimate thing you can do with someone you will never meet. I have leafed through diaries, comforted bereaved spouses and uncovered details that even the family doesn't know.

The resulting stories are neither tribute nor eulogy, nor are they written for the benefit of surviving family members. They are intended to enlighten the reader with anecdotes from a life of interest, giving voice to those who no longer have one. Treat these entries as you might those found in the daily newspaper. Dip into two or three each day, catching up on the passing parade of characters.

Have Christmas dinner in the ruins of an Italian church as enemy shells land nearby; listen to the voice of Casper the Friendly Ghost from Saturday morning cartoons; track the Mad Trapper of Rat River across a frozen mountain pass with a police posse; wince from the blows of police truncheons on the head of labour leader Steve Brodie on Bloody Sunday; laugh at the televised misfortune of a snooker player who split the seat of his pants on national television.

In these pages, death is mere detail. These are tales about how lives were lived.

—*Tom Hawthorn*

ECCENTRICS

Spoony Singh

PROPRIETOR, HOLLYWOOD WAX MUSEUM

(OCTOBER 20, 1922—OCTOBER 18, 2006)

Spoony Singh drove a gold Cadillac and preferred a Nehru jacket to a business suit. Though he was not particularly religious, he wore the turban and full beard of an observant Sikh. Patrons of his Hollywood Wax Museum sometimes mistook the proprietor for an exhibit.

The museum, which opened its doors to a half-mile lineup in January 1965, featured lifelike wax statues of presidents and movie stars, as well as religious figures and famous characters from history. A favourite among the faithful was a tableau depicting Leonardo da Vinci's *The Last Supper*. When a patron complained the museum lacked Jewish heroes, Singh promptly ordered a model of Moses—or, rather, of Charlton Heston as he appeared in *The Ten Commandments*.

Over time, the flamboyant businessman became nearly as famous as some of the stars to be found inside his attraction. He rode an elephant in parades and appeared regularly in gossip columns. "My family left India because we couldn't get enough to eat," he told Hedda Hopper. "Now, I'm paying a doctor to lose weight." Singh let it be known a rising star had not truly achieved a place in the Hollywood firmament until honoured by placement in his museum.

On November 7, 1965, Singh joined a woman who sold dynamite and another who wrote a syndicated sports column as guests on the network television program *What's My Line?* His profession stumped the panel.

He was a showman whose ballyhoo made his museum a great success. The money generated from the tourist attraction built a business empire featuring farming, gold mining and warehousing interests. He also developed property in Mexico and Malibu, the California seaside paradise where he made his home. "I'm making money," he said in a 1970 interview, "and I'm having a ball."

Success was all the more remarkable for his having been born into poverty in India. He grew up on Vancouver Island, where his ambitious plans and prodigious energy built a small fortune, which was soon lost. He recovered, only to suffer as many failures as triumphs before striking it rich in wax. His was a life story worthy of Hollywood.

Sampuran Singh Sundher was born at Kotli, a farming village in the hilly Punjab country of British India. Three years later, the village raised funds to send the family to Canada, a generosity whose motive is today unknown, although the Punjab then, as now, was a place of political and religious turmoil.

The family landed in Vancouver just eleven years after the notorious *Komagata Maru* incident in which a boatload of Sikh immigrants was forced to spend two months at anchor in the harbour before being turned away. The Sundhers settled in Victoria, where his father worked in a sawmill and young "Spoony," as he was nicknamed by classmates, attended Quadra Elementary and Victoria High School.

A quiet segregation in public spaces was reinforced by federal and provincial laws denying Indo-Canadians the franchise, as well as jobs in the civil service, including teaching. Spoony watched movies in Victoria theatres, where he had to sit in the balcony with aboriginal and ethnic-Chinese patrons. Seats on the ground floor were reserved for whites.

His father suffered a business failure and became incapacitated by asthma the summer Spoony graduated from high school. At seventeen, Spoony became the primary breadwinner of a family of six. He found work in a shingle mill, saving money to buy a truck to deliver firewood to homes. He was hired as a foreman at a piecework lumber mill, only to have the day shift walk out to protest having to work for "a Hindu," said his son, Meva Sundher. When Singh was instead assigned to the night shift, his reforms so improved production that day-shift workers asked to work split shifts to reap the benefits.

A shrewd entrepreneur, Singh parlayed this modest beginning into a thriving enterprise. He built Ace Sawmill at Plumper Bay in Esquimalt and operated a logging camp near Port Alberni. He was also responsible for the logging on the north slope of Mount Newton on the Saanich Peninsula north of Victoria. While his son said he had to declare bankruptcy more than once, Singh had enough success by 1954 to build a gracious, four-bedroom private home in the Art Moderne style on Peacock Hill in suburban Saanich. By then, he had married Chanchil Kour Hoti in a union arranged by their families. The pair only agreed to marriage after insisting on going out on chaperoned dates. The residence at 3210 Bellevue Road, no longer in family hands, has been designated a heritage house.

The forestry industry has always been a boom-and-bust business. Singh diversified his interests and satisfied his own fun-loving spirit by opening a roadside amusement park called Spoony's. He offered trampolines for acrobatic guests and built his own go-karts powered by motors scavenged from chainsaws.

While enjoying drinks with his cronies at a Victoria bar, Singh learned of a business opportunity. A former luggage shop and brassiere factory was vacant at 6767 Hollywood Boulevard, just a block east of Grauman's Chinese Theatre and its famous sidewalk with the handprints and footprints of the stars. With the theatre already famous as a draw, the wax museum became a second landmark destination for tourists. Suspecting a better cover story might generate interest, Singh told reporters he opened the museum because he had been shocked on a visit not to have seen any stars on the streets of Hollywood.

The owner was a natural at generating publicity. A 1965 preview offered writers "Bloody Marys and horror d'oeuvres." Another time, he got Louis Armstrong to pose beside a paraffin doppelgänger while blowing a trumpet. The photograph ran in several newspapers. The *Chicago Daily Defender*, with an African-American readership, noted the problem of identification in the caption. "He's on the left . . . no, he's on the right . . . wait a minute, let me think . . . that's the real 'Satchmo' on the left."

Populated mostly by movie stars (Clark Gable, Jean Harlow, Errol Flynn, Mary Pickford, Charlie Chaplin, W.C. Fields, Tallulah Bankhead, Rudolph Valentino), the museum later added more figures from television and pop culture, including Glen Campbell and Sonny and Cher. A figure of Martin Luther King was installed within weeks of his assassination in 1968.

A typical shopping expedition for Singh included purchasing unwanted movie props—an Iron Maiden, a bed of nails and a rubber shark from which protruded a man's leg. He also came to own a pair of pajamas that had belonged to *Playboy* founder Hugh Hefner.

Petty thievery cost the museum about $200 every month, as customers made off with Gandhi's spectacles, Winston Churchill's cigars and Raquel Welch's brassieres. The owner suspected teenagers were responsible. "At that age," he chuckled, "I probably would have done the same thing myself." The four Beatles were displayed behind glass, from which lipstick imprints had to be cleaned before the start of business every day. Despite the security precautions, someone once stole the right hand of drummer Ringo Starr. A wire-service story on the thefts earned Singh far more in publicity than it cost to replace props.

More serious vandalism occurred in 1973, when twenty-nine figures were mutilated overnight. Among the victims were Elton John and six presidents (Grant, Hoover, Truman, Coolidge,

McKinley and Eisenhower). The religious statues were left untouched, as were presidents Nixon and Kennedy. A fire six years later damaged about seventy figures at a cost of more than $250,000 US. The casualties included Stalin and Churchill, as well as Raquel Welch.

With the museum as the anchor of a growing empire, Singh indulged such other interests as gold mining in Mexico and farming in Yuba City, California. He operated warehouses in Thousand Oaks, California; bought the movie theatre across the street from the wax museum, which now operates as the Hollywood Guinness World of Records Museum; and opened a second branch of the Hollywood Wax Museum at Branson, Missouri. The latter includes a faux Mount Rushmore with America's greatest presidents replaced by busts of John Wayne, Elvis Presley, Marilyn Monroe and Charlie Chaplin. This exquisite bit of kitsch was Singh's idea.

Singh befriended many of the stars he immortalized in wax. One he did not get to meet was Marilyn Monroe, who appeared in the museum trying to hold down her white skirt in the famous scene from *The Seven Year Itch*. Singh, a fan of her obvious appeals, particularly enjoyed the whimsical nature of her display. He felt too many patrons left his museum in a sombre state after viewing The Last Supper. It was his long-unfulfilled dream to install a sidewalk air jet at the museum's exit. That, he felt, would have left them laughing.

He died of congestive heart failure at his Malibu home two days before what would have been his eighty-fourth birthday.

October 31, 2006

Bergliot Solberg, known as "The Cougar Lady," takes aim behind her cabin just outside of Sechelt, circa 1995. She and sister Minnie (rear) lived trappers' lives in the back country of the Sunshine Coast. PHOTO PROVIDED BY KEITH THIRKELL

BERGIE SOLBERG

COUGAR LADY

(SEPTEMBER 5, 1923—NOVEMBER 13, 2002)

The body of the Cougar Lady was found on the floor of her shack, where her companion, a dog named Bush, stood lonely vigil for two days. Bergie Solberg was seventy-nine.

Solberg spent her life roaming the mountains and ocean inlets of the Sechelt Peninsula on the Sunshine Coast, surviving on her wiles as a hunter, trapper and logger. A herd of goats provided fresh milk, which she drank raw. The goats also acted as lure for cougars, which she killed.

Ken Collins, a reporter who visited her isolated cabin, tells a story of her fearlessness. Alerted by her dog to the presence of a cougar, an unarmed Solberg chased the wild cat up a tree before returning to her cabin for her rifle. "She was something Walt Disney would like to make a story of," he said. Solberg skinned cougars for their pelts and sold them, as she did those of bobcats and river otters. A deadeye shot at four hundred paces, she patiently tracked quarry for days, scrambling over mountains and pushing through dense underbrush with her head down and shoulders hunched.

Over time, civilization encroached on her seventy-hectare property, a wilderness paradise accessible only by boat. A multimillion-dollar real-estate development was built just two kilometres away. At night, owners of waterfront properties could hear the distinct putt-putt of her boat's 50-hp engine as they lounged in hot tubs. Her own shack lacked electricity and running water.

"There's not many animals left," she once complained to reporter Keith Thirkell. "Many people are moving to Sechelt, building houses, and more people are sport hunting, which scares away the game."

After the death of her older sister, she was a last living reminder of a celebrated way of life otherwise confined to memory and history books.

Herman Solberg, a logger from Norway, moved his wife, Olga, and two daughters, Minnie and Bergliot Asta, to Sandy Hook on the peninsula in 1928. Bergie, as she was called, and Minnie joined their father in the woods, learning the dangerous job of logging. She took over her father's trapping permit after his death, selling mink and raccoon pelts to city furriers.

The Solberg sisters lived alone. They had little use for the conveniences of the modern age, preferring the solitary independence of the old-time homesteader. They spoke to one another in Norwegian and their English carried the accent of a homeland they could barely remember.

Over the years, Minnie Solberg settled in at an old logging camp at Deserted Bay. The closest store was fifty kilometres away. The sisters were not an uncommon sight in Sechelt, visiting monthly for provisions. Bergie Solberg wore a heavy purple cowboy hat, the weight of which left the tops of her ears bent like a terrier. She dressed in heavy sweaters and other thrift-shop fashions. Many in town thought her a recluse, yet she was no hermit. Some years ago, she was profiled by a European television crew, making her better known in France than in her own country. Reporters who visited her shack were treated to tea served on china, or offered a rusty can of soda pop.

Collins once joined her on a hunting expedition. He recalled her spotting cougar scat. "Like a connoisseur rolling a favoured Cuban cigar with her fingers," he wrote, "she fondled the piece of feces, broke it in half, and put it to her nose, inhaling deeply." She pronounced it fresh, before describing the cougar's diet. Asked to pose for a photograph, she stood atop a stump and slung her bolt-action carbine over her shoulder, grasping the barrel with her left hand.

Her rifle once got her into trouble with a local conservation officer, who served her papers explaining hunting regulations, and once reportedly tried to seize her firearm. Solberg did not know how to read, the reporter said, and had a difficult time understanding the concept of seasons for hunting. If she saw game, he said, it was in season.

Her home was jerry-built from pieces of wood scavenged over the years. Her many possessions were piled high against the walls "in case," she said, "there's ever shortages again—like during the war."

Solberg stayed in contact with the outside world through a citizen's band radio. (Her handle was Cougar Lady.) When a friend was unable to reach her over two days, another friend was dispatched to the shack, where her body was found. Sechelt RCMP said she died of natural causes. Her friends suspect she suffered a stroke, as there was evidence that she collapsed midway through preparing a meal.

December 14, 2002

Ian Hunter

"HIGH PRIEST OF POT"

(MARCH 20, 1961—AUGUST 14, 2002)

Ian Hunter called himself a reverend for the Church of the Universe. He claimed to be on a "Mission of Ecstasy" and described cannabis as a sacrament. The evangelist for marijuana, who brought to his advocacy a wit and flair unappreciated by those who upheld the laws he challenged, died in an accidental drowning on Kootenay Lake, aged forty-one.

Acting as his own lawyer on three drug-related offences in 1998, he told a BC Supreme Court justice that since the constitution recognizes the supremacy of God, and since God created marijuana plants, therefore all anti-marijuana laws were unconstitutional. The judge dismissed the challenge and ordered him to stand trial.

After conviction and the imposition of a $500 fine, Hunter remained unrepentant about promoting marijuana. "I carry some with me all the time," he said. "I consider it my sacred duty as a minister, like a medicine man."

Hunter was a rebel with a cause and the newspapers called him a "hemp honcho" and a "high priest of pot."

With nineteenth-century mutton chop sideburns and pristine white suit, Hunter cast a dandy Beau Brummell figure when campaigning for mayor of Victoria in 1996. The suit was made of hemp fibre. He finished a distant third, though he proved more popular than five other candidates.

Ian Fergus Hunter was born in New Westminster to an insurance agent and a mother who had polio. He learned journalism at the *Other Press*, the student newspaper at Douglas College. At twenty-three, he became editor of the *Squamish Times* and later contributed to Vancouver radio station CFRO, known as Co-op Radio.

In 1988, he produced a provocative report for CBC Radio's *Ideas* program advocating the vote for children. Hunter noted that arguments once used to deny the franchise to women and people of colour were also cited to keep children from the ballot box. He contributed a seven-page statement outlining his position on children's suffrage to the Royal Commission on Electoral Reform and Party Financing in 1991.

He had first become publicly identified as a marijuana advocate in the early 1990s when he opened the Hemp BC store near Victory Square in Vancouver with Marc Emery. They called their budding business "capitalist activism."

In 1993, when Prime Minister Kim Campbell admitted to having smoked marijuana, Hunter tried to present her with a certificate declaring her "a research associate in our hemp-cultivation program." Tongue firmly in cheek, Hunter said his group was called the Institute for Adversarial Irony.

After moving to Victoria, Hunter opened his own hemp store called the Sacred Herb near city hall. He also initiated weekly marijuana smoke-ins at Beacon Hill Park, which attracted from fifty to a hundred and fifty aficionados. Victoria police broke up one of the protests in May 1996, charging three people with possession. Hunter wanted eleven police officers to be charged with obstructing a religious service, but the Crown said there was no reasonable chance of conviction.

Two months later, police raided his store and Hunter was charged with trafficking marijuana seeds, growing a marijuana plant, and possession of a small amount of psilocybin, so-called magic mushrooms.

When Justice Montague Drake dismissed Hunter's constitutional challenge, he noted that marijuana seemed to be his church's only dogma. Hunter was later convicted by a jury and fined by the judge. An appeal was rejected by a 3–0 vote by the BC Court of Appeal. Hunter vowed to take his case to the Supreme Court of Canada, but lacked funds to pay for a transcript of his trial.

Meanwhile, police asked council to review the store's business licence. Council voted 6–3 to revoke the licence, the deciding vote for the two-thirds majority necessary cast by the mayor, Bob Cross, against whom Hunter had campaigned two years earlier.

He sold his store and eventually moved to Nelson, where he co-hosted a weekly, two-hour radio program called *Fane of the Cosmos Infinite Moment*. (Fane is an archaic word for temple.) The other host was Dustin Cantwell, proprietor of the Holy Smoke Culture Shop.

"He always pushed ideas," Cantwell told Pot-TV, an Internet broadcaster. "You'd have an idea and he'd bat it into the outfield."

Hunter also explored a variety of New Age practices, including yoga and tai chi. When he was first reported missing, six friends cast the I Ching before launching a search. His body was found floating in Kootenay Lake near a small powerboat. The RCMP said he had accidentally drowned, although no witnesses were available to describe the circumstances.

September 30, 2002

ENTERTAINERS

In 1931, Harvey Lowe, a boy of thirteen from Victoria proclaimed to be the world yo-yo champion and demonstrated his skill with the stringed toy for a London audience including Amelia Earhart and the Prince of Wales. He later found a wider audience by showing off his skill on the television variety show, The Smothers Brothers Comedy Hour. Lowe's brush with Hollywood included a request by the director Robert Altman to teach Julie Christie the proper technique for smoking opium. PHOTO COURTESY OF THE ESTATE OF HARVEY LOWE

HARVEY LOWE

WORLD YO-YO CHAMPION

(OCTOBER 30, 1918—MARCH 11, 2009)

Little Harvey Lowe's mastery of a simple, ordinary toy—the yo-yo—became his passport to a boyhood adventure that would make him a world champion. He wore proudly for the rest of his days a title won at age thirteen.

In his nimble hands, the yo-yo became more than a child's plaything.

He handled the string like a puppet master, causing his yo-yo to spin, dance, and, in the nomenclature of the pastime, sleep. He claimed a repertoire of a thousand tricks. On rare occasion, he performed a feat in which a pair of wooden yo-yos whipped within a blink of his face. He called this the death-defying Mandarin puzzle, a reminder of the toy's origins as a hunting weapon in the Philippines.

As an adult, Lowe appeared on stage at clubs as one of the entertainments in an era when a venue's nightly attractions might include a half-dozen acts. He later appeared on television, most notably on the *Smothers Brothers Comedy Hour*, for which he wore an elaborate robe in his role as a Confucius Yomaster. It was his job to teach the venerable art to a character portrayed by Tommy Smothers called Yo-Yo Man.

Away from the stage and screen, Lowe acted as an unofficial ambassador to Vancouver's Chinatown, with all its attendant mysteries. It once fell to him, for instance, to educate the actress Julie Christie in the proper technique for smoking opium.

Earlier, he had become the first Chinese-Canadian to host a radio show.

Willing to indulge ballyhoo to promote his craft, Lowe professed a belief in the spiritual depth of playing with a toy on a string. "There is a definite Zen spirit to the yo-yo," he once told newspaper columnist Denny Boyd. "It's just wood and string and it occupies a tiny space in your hand. When you release it, you free its spirit and create vibrations that come back to you."

Named Lowe Kwong Yoi at his birth in Victoria in 1918, just twelve days before the end of the Great War, he was the youngest of ten children born to Lowe Gee Quai, born in China, and Seto Ming Yook, born in Victoria. His father, known as Charlie Lowe, was one of three brothers to establish tailor shops on Government Street in Victoria. The boy was raised in a household overseen by his biological mother, but the woman who most looked after him was his father's concubine, he told reporter John Mackie. "Imagine, both of them were living under the same roof. But they got along good," he said.

At twelve, he bought his first yo-yo for thirty-five cents. He soon mastered the novelty, the popularity of which was promoted by neighbourhood contests. Young Harvey won these, graduating to showdowns at department stores. Continued success led to invitations to compete in Vancouver, where he again defeated all comers. Irving Cook, a promoter, took the boy overseas as a yo-yo craze swept Britain in 1932.

A yo-yo demonstration performed at the Derby Ball at Grosvenor House in London on June 1 was witnessed by the American aviatrix Amelia Earhart and by the Prince of Wales, heir to the throne. The prince even tried his hand at the toy.

At the Empire Theatre on London's Leicester Square, Harvey Lowe faced a dozen young challengers representing rival yo-yo manufacturers in a showdown demanding skill, innovation and, as it turned out, a bit of luck.

Lowe was one of three competitors from Canada sponsored by the Cheerio company, which was promoting its No. 99 yo-yo. The other two, both from Regina, were Gene Mauk and Joe Young, the reigning world champion. In the finals, Young's string snapped, while Lowe was able to complete his performance without mishap. He was crowned world champion a month before his fourteenth birthday. With the crown came £1,500.

Though born in Canada to a Canadian-born mother, Lowe was said to represent China in the competition.

He then toured England and France. "I was wearing a white tie and tails," he said. "I played at the Café de Paris, a real nightclub."

During the tour, the promoter paid his mother $25 a month, while the boy received $1.25 a day in meal money. He had earlier won a bicycle, which to his boyhood eyes was the equal to having a Cadillac of his own. It was said his hands had been insured by Lloyd's of London for £100,000, a fact dutifully repeated by newspapers. Left unreported was the duration of the policy, believed to have been a single day.

He returned home to Victoria for high school. Then, his mother wanted her son to go to China. "You've got a Chinese face," she told him, "you've got to learn Chinese." So he joined an older married sister in Shanghai, where he studied business at St. John's University. Not long after his arrival, the Japanese seized the city, beginning a brutal seven-year occupation. He managed to skirt between two worlds as an ethnic Chinese whose nationality did not make him an enemy until December 1941.

Lowe was enlisted as a spy by Japanese intelligence, he once told *Ricepaper*, a Vancouver-based magazine, though he protected his friends and deliberately misled his handlers. He otherwise described a high-living wartime spent riding in Italian sports cars and going to jazz clubs. It was during the war that he became a broadcaster, reading English news reports on a station owned by his wealthy brother-in-law. He became a celebrity, his popularity peaking after the war. Lowe returned to British Columbia after the Communists took over the city.

By then fluently bilingual, Lowe was hired as a doorman by a club in Vancouver. Corrupt authorities turned a blind eye to gambling by Chinese Canadians, though not necessarily to lawbreaking by those of European ancestry. It was his job to ensure only bona fide club members entered the premises.

He sought work at local radio stations. Eventually, CJOR agreed to air *The Call of China*, a pioneering thirty-minute program that aired on Sunday afternoons.

"We tried to deal with everything authentically Chinese," Lowe told a student publication in 1985. "I might be talking about pagodas, and I'd do research on that. Between each segment, I'd play a lot of Chinese music. There were more Canadian listeners than Chinese because the program was directed more toward them." The show, believed to be the first in Canada with a Chinese-Canadian host, launched in 1951 and remained on the air for fourteen years.

Lowe became a prominent figure in Chinatown. In 1958, a Liberal senator contemptuously referred to Douglas Jung, a Member of Parliament from Vancouver, as "this Chinaman." As president of the Chinatown chapter of the Lions Club, Lowe defended the MP, noting the senator's words were "a great insult" and "objectionable because of its association with race prejudice."

Lowe continued to perform with his yo-yos at such venues as the grand Orpheum Theatre and the bamboo-decorated Marco Polo nightclub, where he was stage manager. In 1971, the director Robert Altman asked Lowe to round up one hundred ethnic Chinese as extras for a movie he was shooting in West Vancouver with the working title, *The Presbyterian Church Wager*. Lowe enlisted friends, family and restaurant customers for a scene that, alas, wound up on the cutting-room floor when the film, retitled *McCabe & Mrs. Miller*, was released in 1971. He is credited in the movie in a role as a townsman.

It was during the filming that the actress Julie Christie, a noted perfectionist, asked Lowe to show her the proper technique for the ingestion of opium. Though he had never used the narcotic himself, he consulted old-timers in Chinatown and got the information.

May 12, 2009

A stage actress from Vancouver, Norma Macmillan became the sound of countless Saturday mornings as the voice of such animated cartoon characters as Sweet Polly Purebred and Casper the Friendly Ghost. In 1962, she provided the voices of Caroline and John-John for the best-selling comedy album, "The First Family," which poked fun at the Kennedys. PHOTO COURTESY OF THE ESTATE OF NORMA MACMILLAN

NORMA MACMILLAN

VOICE OF CASPER THE FRIENDLY GHOST

(SEPTEMBER 15, 1921—MARCH 16, 2001)

Norma Macmillan was the voice of countless Saturday mornings, her acting skill making real for children the vulnerability of such cartoon characters as Sweet Polly Purebred and Casper the Friendly Ghost.

A short woman with a pixie face, Macmillan was known for her sharp wit and determination both in private and in performance. She appeared in more than a hundred stage productions before becoming a voice for cartoon and animated characters with credits including such 1960s staples as *Underdog*, *The Gumby Show* and *Davey and Goliath*.

In her later years, Macmillan took on bit roles as an actor. She performed with Katharine Hepburn in the 1986 made-for-TV movie *Mrs. Delafield Wants to Marry*; was hacked to death by axe in *Nightmare on the 13th Floor* (1990); and portrayed a bumbling nurse who mixed up two sets of twin girls in *Big Business*, a 1988 comedy starring Bette Midler and Lily Tomlin.

A doctor's daughter born in Vancouver, she attended Prince of Wales and York House schools before graduating from Trinity College in London. She met her future husband, producer Thor

Arngrim, while working on a production for the groundbreaking Totem Theatre in her hometown. They were married in 1954.

They became a celebrated Hollywood couple. Arngrim was personal manager to Liberace and Debbie Reynolds, among other clients, while also handling the careers of their children, Stefan Arngrim (Barry Lockridge in *Land of the Giants*) and Alison Arngrim (Nellie Oleson on *Little House on the Prairie*).

While her voice work and movie acting earned the praise of her peers, the public recognized Macmillan mostly as an actor in commercials. She was cast as a dotty, flighty and angry senior for such clients as the Yellow Pages (as Alice Rootweevil) and Kraft Mayonnaise (as Aunt Martha), whose memorable, if annoying, slogan was a tart "It's creamier!"

It was her special talent to make a two-dimensional cartoon character seem a flesh-and-blood human. The nuance of her voice expressed a child's playfulness, pugnaciousness and vulnerability.

One of her early children's roles was as the voice of Fitzgerald Fieldmouse, a puppet friend of the title character on *Maggie Muggins*, a fifteen-minute, after-school program that ran from 1955 to 1962 on CBC Television.

She performed the voice of Kokette to Larry Storch's Koko the Clown in a hundred animated short cartoons.

Macmillan's incarnation of the friendly ghost captured the lonely spirit of a boy whose disembodied nature too often scared away those he wished to befriend.

On the *Gumby* series, an early Claymation effort featuring the adventures of a green clay boy and his pink clay horse, Macmillan was the voice of Goo, a blue blob and a rare female presence. She also voiced Gumby for a few seasons.

In *Davey and Goliath* (1962), Macmillan handled the voice chores of Davey, a brown-haired boy in tidy slacks and a red-striped shirt whose curiosity got him into minor scrapes. Goliath, voiced by Hal Smith, who portrayed Otis the Drunk on *The Andy Griffith Show*, was Davey's dim-witted conscience, whose trademark was a cautionary "But Da-a-a-a-vey."

The show blazed a progressive path by portraying Davey's best friend as a black boy at a time when few black characters of any kind were seen on television. The boys' racial difference was unremarked upon save for a single episode titled "Difference" that offered a lesson in tolerance.

The makers of *The Simpsons* acknowledge the show's pop-culture status by occasionally incorporating a reference such as having the doorbell at the Flanders' house play the *Davey and Goliath* theme song.

Macmillan was already the best-known child's voice in the United States when she was cast to play the role of US President John F. Kennedy's children, Caroline and baby John-John, for a comedy album starring little-known comic Vaughn Meader. *The First Family*, mild satire by today's standards, gently poked at the foibles of a young president's family. The album struck a funny bone in middle America in the late fall of 1962, selling more than seven million copies in two months.

Macmillan posed for the album's cover in a pink gingham dress with bared arms and legs, a pink barrette in her hair, a sun bonnet on her head, holding a yellow balloon.

Kennedy's assassination a year later abruptly ended Meader's comedy career. By then, Macmillan had already returned to the sound booth.

Another of her memorable animated television characters was Sweet Polly Purebred, a TV reporter in peril who called upon her boyfriend Underdog (Wally Cox) to rescue her from such evil-doers as Riff Raff and evil scientist Simon Bar Sinister, who wanted citizens to do as "Simon says." *Underdog*, a mild parody of *Superman*, ran from 1964 until 1973, making Macmillan's voice familiar as Polly Purebread crying, "Oh where, oh where has my Underdog gone? Oh where, oh where can he be?"

Her voice can be heard on many other cartoon series, including as Li'LRok in *Moby Dick and Mighty Mightor*, as well as on many animated commercials. She was heard by another generation of children doing miscellaneous voices for cartoon episodes of the *Smurfs* and *Go Bots*.

Much less well known was her work as a playwright. *A Crowded Affair*, a witty exposé of social mores in a privileged Vancouver milieu written in the style of Noel Coward, is credited as the first play with a British Columbia setting to have been written by a woman. Macmillan also wrote *Free As a Bird*, a screwball, Cold War comedy that starred the Tony Award-winning comedienne Edie Adams.

She returned to her Vancouver birthplace in 1994, hosting a weekly program for seniors on Co-op Radio.

For many years, she worked on a novel, a multigenerational saga in the style of *The Thorn Birds*, beginning at the moment of contact between the indigenous peoples and the Europeans. She'd visit Vancouver Island for inspiration, staying in isolated cabins, a glass of Scotch beside her trusted Olivetti portable typewriter. (At home, she preferred a large bag of popcorn.)

Macmillan got a literary agent, had a mockup of the book constructed and shopped it around. The British television host David Frost found it cinematic in structure, and there was some interest expressed in turning it into a movie, or television series. But, as is so often the nature of these things, nothing happened.

On her death, her family came across a box filled with a typescript on sheaves of the cheapest newsprint in pink, green and beige, a literary spumoni. Arngrim vowed to get the novel published.

Nine years later, after substantial revisions by the journalist Charles Campbell, TouchWood Editions of Victoria released *The Maquinna Line: A Family Saga*. The reviews were favourable.

Arngrim was in the intensive-care unit at St. Paul's Hospital, battling Parkinson's disease, when presented a colour copy of the cover for his late wife's novel. He did not live long enough to see the finished product, but died knowing he had fulfilled a promise.

April 3, 2001

Billy Cowsill

SINGER AND SONGWRITER
(JANUARY 9, 1948—FEBRUARY 17, 2006)

Billy Cowsill's voice captured the anguish of the accused, the pain of the broken-hearted and the frustration of the unrequited lover.

He first won an audience as the lead singer of the family group The Cowsills, who had a trio of Top 10 hits in the late 1960s. He launched the band with three of his look-alike brothers, but it was his father's insistence on including a little sister and their mother that made the Cowsills a novelty act and the inspiration for the later television series, *The Partridge Family*.

Cowsill resented the addition of other family members. He wanted to lead a rock group and did not particularly care to be the front man of a wholesome family band. The Cowsills became a target for critics of manufactured pop music in part because of a squeaky-clean image reinforced by an advertising campaign for milk.

Though the Cowsills produced bubblegum pop, the group deserved greater respect for pleasing harmonies evocative of the Beach Boys and the Everly Brothers.

Cowsill left the group in 1971 to embark on an unsuccessful solo career, eventually settling in Canada. He found redemption

Billy Cowsill enjoys a smoke outside Calgary's Mecca Cafe in 2002. He hit the pop charts with three Top 10 tunes as lead singer of the Cowsills, the family act that was the model for television's Partridge Family. PHOTO PROVIDED BY THE CALGARY HERALD ARCHIVES

through live performances in small clubs and the admiration of other musicians.

Those who caught any of his innumerable dates in those years were treated to a singer who could rave on like Buddy Holly, or be as lonely as Roy Orbison. On classic country tunes, at which he was peerless, he sounded like Hank Williams as channelled through George Jones.

A variety of addictions and a tendency toward self-destruction kept him from wider acclaim. Critics found much to praise in his later work, particularly the recorded work of his Blue Shadows, a brilliant Vancouver country-rock quartet Cowsill once described as "three vegetarians and a junkie." After moving to Calgary, he formed a group called the Co-Dependents, whose two releases of live music have been well received. He had talent, but he also had demons. He was, in many ways, a survivor of an unforgiving father and a heartless music industry.

Billy Cowsill grew up the eldest child of a US Navy sailor. His father, William (Bud) Cowsill, spent six months at a time at sea, yet managed with wife Barbara to produce offspring in rapid succession: Billy, 1948; twins Richard and Robert, 1950; Paul, 1952; Barry, 1955, John, 1956; Susan, 1960. The boys shared a gap-toothed grin and jet-black hair.

The peripatetic family changed zip codes almost as often as they changed diapers, as Bud's postings took them from New England to Virginia to California, and back again.

"One of my first memories is when I'm three or four years old, my dad bringing me into a beer joint and just popping me in front of the Wurlitzer jukebox," Billy Cowsill once told me. "All he had to do was keep the quarters coming."

Unfortunately, Bud Cowsill came from a troubled family. "He was a real good guy, a guy who would give you the shirt off his back," Billy Cowsill said. "But if he'd got a gut full of liquor, he'd beat your head into the wall."

Retiring from the navy in 1963, Bud Cowsill settled his large brood at Newport, RI. A hustler by nature, and struggling on an inadequate pension, the family was so poor they chopped up furniture for the fireplace after being cut off from heating oil. They also neglected to shovel the driveway in an attempt to discourage bill collectors. When his sons formed a band, Bud Cowsill eagerly followed a neighbour's suggestion of putting the children on stage.

Led by Billy, the Cowsill boys had put together a quartet, a reflection of the family's insular nature after years on the road. None had formal musical training. With Billy on guitar, Bob on guitar and organ, Barry on bass, and John on drums, the young quartet played church socials, school sock hops and weddings.

At one gig they were spotted by a holidaying writer for *The Today Show* and they soon made their network television debut. After that, success was assured for "America's First Family of Music," whose lineup often included the boys' mother, Barbara, and sister Susan. The band's hit singles included *The Rain, The Park, and Other Things* (1967), *Indian Lake* (1968) and *Hair* (1969), the title song of the rock musical. Five other singles also reached the charts in those years, a stunning reversal of fortune for the family.

They lost it almost as suddenly. Bud Cowsill, who was the group's business manager, filed for bankruptcy in 1975, owing about $450,000 to creditors.

Billy Cowsill had long since left the band. He had an explosive argument with his father in Las Vegas and was fired the next day.

A Cowsill by name but no longer by profession, he recorded a solo album that sank without a trace and then wandered across America, playing in coffee shops and taverns. Along the way, the Beach Boys invited him on tour to replace Brian Wilson, who had suffered a nervous breakdown. Cowsill decided to seek out his hero before taking the gig. By then, the corpulent Beach Boy had retired into a world of his own making that included a sandbox in his living room.

"Oh, Billy, don't do it," Wilson warned. "It'll drive you crazy. It'll get you nuts."

Cowsill followed his idol's advice. "I looked at him and thought ... obviously this guy knows what he's talking about."

Instead, he used the last of his Cowsills money to buy a bar in Austin, Texas. As might be predicted, he and his coterie drank the joint dry. Cowsill headed north, stopping in the Northwest Territories, where he found work driving trucks from Hay River over the frozen Great Slave Lake to Yellowknife.

By 1979, he had landed in Vancouver, where he fronted Blue Northern, producing a four-song extended-play record in 1980 and an album the following year.

He continued to drink heavily until the birth of a son inspired him to stop. It was a short-lived abstinence. He would later joke he had considered writing a song titled, "How Can I Look up to Daddy When He's Passed Out on the Floor?"

One of the highlights of his live performances was a Dead Man's Set, in which Cowsill and his band would play only tunes by deceased rock stars.

Larry Wanagas, who was singer k.d. lang's manager, brought Cowsill into his stable, but was unable to get him aligned with a record label. "No one would sign me because my name was Cowsill," he once complained. "For three years, if I was a space heater, [Wanagas] couldn't have sold me to the Eskimos."

Cowsill was about to move to Nashville when he hooked up with Jeffrey Hatcher, a prolific tunesmith with whom he formed The Blue Shadows. The rocking country outfit called their ringing harmonies "Hank Williams goes to the Cavern Club." Their 1993 debut album, *On the Floor of Heaven*, won a Juno nomination for country group of the year. They followed with a second album, *Lucky To Me*, which also won critical acclaim, but once again proved too country for rock radio and too rock for country radio. The group dissolved in 1996.

Cowsill suffered from a serious back problem, an injury whose pain he tried to mask with ever more serious bouts of drinking and pill popping. Friends brought him to Calgary, where he once again went on the wagon and underwent back surgery. Despite a deteriorating physical condition, Cowsill continued to perform, even taking to the stage despite needing a cane following hip-replacement surgery.

His death, while sudden, was not entirely unexpected. Cowsill was known to suffer from emphysema, osteoporosis and Cushing's syndrome, a hormonal imbalance. The news reached his surviving siblings as they gathered in Rhode Island to mark the death of brother Barry Cowsill in New Orleans. He had gone missing in Hurricane Katrina in September 2005, and his body was not identified until the following January. A day after their older brother's death, the surviving Cowsills recreated their sunny sound at a memorial service.

February 28, 2006

Alberta Slim

YODELING COWBOY SINGER

(FEBRUARY 2, 1910—NOVEMBER 25, 2005)

Pearl Edwards

PEARL THE ELEPHANT GIRL

(OCTOBER 7, 1922—MARCH 18, 2006)

Best known as the singer Alberta Slim, Eric Edwards was an English-born yodeling cowboy who rode the rails of Western Canada during the Depression, stopping along the way to coax coins for his supper from passersby by singing hobo songs on street corners.

After he built a career as a western singer on radio in Saskatchewan, he returned to touring the country, both as a singer and with his own travelling circus. On one such barnstorming journey through the Maritimes, he was inspired by a fragrant springtime phenomenon to write *When It's Apple Blossom Time in the Annapolis Valley*.

That song would become his signature. Edwards's verse was simple in construction and heartfelt in delivery. He performed until 2003 when, at ninety-three, a variety of infirmities at last made it impossible for him to follow the open road.

An irrepressible performer, Edwards had a predilection for cowboy shirts and white stetsons. He never willingly surrendered a microphone. He was, by his own admission, a yodeling fool, as likely to launch into an extended call in the middle of conversation

Alberta Slim began his country music career during the Depression by hopping on freight trains and singing for his supper. He played and toured until 2003 when, at age ninety-three, he could no longer travel to perform. PHOTO COURTESY OF THE CALGARY PUBLIC LIBRARY, COMMUNITY HERITAGE AND FAMILY HISTORY DIGITAL LIBRARY as he was to do in song. "That yodeling don't go with it," he said with a whoop on one such occasion. "I just did it for the hell of it."

Eric Charles Edwards was born at Wilsford, Wiltshire, a village near Salisbury Plain in England. His father, who drove a taxi and ran a pool hall, moved the family to nearby Upavon after returning from service in the Great War. While working as a publican at Larkhill, the descriptions of Canada by homesick Canadian soldiers billeted in the area persuaded him to immigrate to a land he had never seen.

The Edwards family purchased three quarter-sections of ranchland near the Saskatchewan side of Lloydminster in 1920. A move to St. Walburg came two years later. Music provided entertainment at home, as father fiddled and mother played an organ, while the four boys and three girls joined in on banjo and guitar.

The cowboy crooner left home as a young man with a guitar and $25 raised from selling his horse to a neighbouring rancher. He hopped a train to Edmonton, where he bought three guitar lessons before auditioning at a local radio station. While awaiting word on the job, he wandered the streets, stumbling across an old man playing a whistle pipe who invited him to join in. It was the first but not the last time he would eat thanks to busking.

The radio station did not hire him. Instead, a sympathetic staffer put him in touch with an English couple whose attempts at homesteading had failed and who were desperate enough to revive a career as entertainers. They bought a four-door touring car and hit the road with their twelve-year-old son and the yodeling cowboy. They earned blessed little, and the boy and the singer were often reduced to stealing vegetables from private gardens. The unlikely foursome called it quits when the couple could not afford the $30 monthly payments for the car.

Edwards spent the Depression years blowing across the country like a tumbleweed, courtesy of the freight trains on which he hitched an unpaid ride. He took to sidewalks to sing songs such as *Waiting for a Train* when he needed to fill an empty belly.

In 1937, he had a meeting with a store owner that would take him off the streets. Broke and hungry on arrival in Regina, he headed for the Salvation Army, as the Sally Ann "always had a meal for us and a flop in a dormitory." He learned from the hobo grapevine that the Army and Navy Store sponsored a half-hour amateur show on radio station CKCK. The only payment was a free breakfast, reward enough for hungry men.

The singer went to the store, told the owner he intended to perform on the show, and asked for clothes to replace the rags he was wearing. Sam Cohen outfitted him with a pair of pants. The singer's rendition of Wilf Carter's *There's a Love Knot in My Lariat* won him an offer to be a daily regular on the show.

He earned money for room and board at the Regina Café, where he was allowed to pass the hat after each performance. He also earned tips by reading tea leaves. One day, he gazed into the drained cup of a nineteen-year-old farm girl and predicted that Pearl Griffin would become his wife. In this one instance, at least, he was presceint.

Pearl Evelyn Griffin was born in Lestock, a small community in south-central Saskatchewan, about a hundred kilometres west of Yorktown. Her family traced its roots on the prairie to John Pritchard, an early Red River settler. Pearl was the sixth of seven children born to a midwife and a drayman. Her father supported the family during the Depression by holding five jobs.

She left the village for Star City, located nearer Saskatoon. There, she moved in with relatives to complete Grade 12, which was not offered in her hometown. The local telephone exchange was set up in the home, so she worked as an operator to pay for her room and board.

She soon found similar work in Regina. It was on her first day off that she joined a friend at a downtown café where a cowboy singer made his bold prediction of marriage. They married two years later in 1943 and for the duration of their union the bride addressed her husband as Slim.

Edwards had taken the name years earlier while on the road as a yodeling cowboy. He had a partner, a singer who called himself

Alberta Slim, who enlisted in the armed forces when war broke out in 1939.

As Edwards recalled, "The guys on the freight all joined up. They wanted to eat. Me, I didn't want to fight. He gave me all his clothes. I started wearing his silk shirts with Alberta Slim written across the back. They began calling me Alberta Slim and that's the way I got it. Never saw him again. I heard through folks he was killed overseas."

Edwards was hired by station CFQC in Saskatoon to perform a fifteen-minute show three mornings each week for a princely $4.50. After four months, his workweek and payment were doubled. He supplemented his income by offering listeners a chance to purchase a publicity photograph. He was not permitted to sell the pictures over the air; instead, he asked ten cents for shipping and handling. He got a bag of mail each day and soon had enough money to buy a trick horse with which he would perform at local rodeo shows, appearances that he would promote over the radio. After four years, he moved his act to CKRM in Regina.

Edwards performed on the radio in winter and followed the carnival circuit in summer. He had a 350-person tent, a backup band called the Bar X Boys, and a trick horse named Kitten. The horse had a repertoire of stunts, including knot untying and kneeling in prayer. For what was called the automobile act, she rested on her back while Edwards sat on her belly holding a front hoof in each hand, as though steering.

At each show, a young girl from the audience was brought before Kitten. Asked how many children she would bear, the horse would slowly paw at the dirt, until the crowd collapsed in laughter as the count reached thirteen, fourteen and sometimes fifteen.

The travelling menagerie eventually included Babe the singing dog, Blackie the high-diving dog, and Butch the walking Dalmatian, who could traverse 400 metres on his hind legs while carrying a 2.5-metre pole balanced on his front paws. Pearl Edwards performed in the circus as a featured attraction billed as "Pearl the Elephant Girl." Dressed in frilly costumes of her own design and making, her act included standing on the shoulders of a rearing elephant named Susie. The talented pachyderm was also capable of playing the harmonica, a skill that eluded her biped partner.

Edwards moved his radio show to CKNW in New Westminster in 1947, when much of the listening audience on the outskirts of Vancouver was still living a rural life. He began recording in Toronto in 1949 for RCA Victor, releasing singles and albums on the Camden label. Many of his compositions were also recorded by other artists, including *My Nova Scotia Home, My Fraser Valley Home* and *Beautiful British Columbia*. He had a penchant for Wilf Carter tunes, several of which can be found on his recordings. A man whose livelihood had depended on keeping abreast of technological change—from radio to 78 rpm records to 33⅓ vinyl to cassettes to compact discs—was not cowed by the computer age. Alberta Slim sold music online from his personal website.

Edwards and his wife moved to New Westminster outside Vancouver in 1947, later settling on the south side of the Fraser River in Surrey. They wintered in British Columbia and spent their summers criss-crossing the nation.

The couple decided to abandon their itinerant life after the birth of their second child. The circus critters were sold, save for Kitten Jr., which was taught a repertoire of tricks in the family's basement. The colt performed at charity functions.

Alberta Slim continued to record and perform, while Pearl Edwards operated the family's Bar X Motel on the King George Highway. The couple also operated a mortgage brokerage business known as Bar X Enterprises, through which they purchased, improved and resold residential properties.

Every August, Pearl returned briefly to her former carnie life by working the midway at the Pacific National Exhibition in Vancouver. Her game was Duck Pond, in which a small prize was guaranteed all players. It was her particular skill to encourage fathers and boyfriends to spend large sums—one quarter at a time—in an effort to win a large stuffed animal.

A year before his death, Alberta Slim released a cassette tape including a new composition, *The Phantom of Whistler Mountain*, to celebrate the awarding of the 2010 Winter Olympics.

While cowboy music fell out of style long ago, Edwards enjoyed a revival in recent years for his dedication to an almost-lost form. His ninety-second birthday was celebrated at the Railway Club, a hipster hangout in Vancouver. He also performed at the Vancouver Folk Music Festival and the Stan Rogers Folk Festival in Canso, Nova Scotia. A display honouring Edwards can be found at the Apple Capital Museum in Berwick, Nova Scotia, in the heart of the Annapolis Valley. In 2003, he received a lifetime achievement award from the BC Country Music Association.

That same year, he appeared on the main stage at Rootsfest in Sidney, north of Victoria. His appearance at a workshop with Amy Sky, Stephen Fearing and John Mann of Spirit of the West was notable for the enthusiasm of Edwards's yodeling. His white hair cascading past his shoulders, a cowboy hat on his head, he yodeled until he was nearly hoarse, as though he knew time was limited and he had better yodel while he could.

December 6, 2005

JOHN JULIANI

THEATRE DIRECTOR, FOUNDER OF SAVAGE GOD

(MARCH 24, 1940—AUGUST 21, 2003)

John Juliani was a provocateur in life as on stage. A man passionate about the possibilities of theatre, he roused reverence in some, antipathy in others.

His most infamous act was to challenge the Stratford Festival's newly hired artistic director to a duel. Robin Phillips's offence was that he was British when Juliani and others were certain a land as grand as Canada was capable of producing a director for its Shakespearean theatre. What he called a "romantic gesture with tongue in cheek" earned cheers from Canadian theatre directors and sneers from much of the theatre establishment.

Juliani was an unabashed Canadian nationalist, a dedicated fan of the avant garde, an ardent defender of the right of actors to a decent living, a champion of playwright George Ryga and a tireless figure so commanding as to develop an intense loyalty among acolytes.

At the same time, he was seen as a kook, a dilettante and a street fighter. One critic called him "the Tiger Williams of Canadian theatre," his pugnacious approach earning him comparison to a notorious hockey goon. In his defence, Juliani explained that he was merely a "true believer" with opinions on controversial subjects.

Juliani's credits were long and varied, including spontaneous sixties street happenings such as the staging of his own wedding as a theatrical performance and brief appearances on such 1990s television dramas as *The X-Files*.

From 1982 until 1997, Juliani was executive producer of radio drama for CBC Radio in Vancouver. He helped to bring to air many celebrated productions, including the provocative *Dim Sum Diaries* by playwright Mark Leiren-Young.

Juliani also possessed a head-turning beauty with a profile as striking as a Roman bust. Radio host Bill Richardson commented on his handsomeness at a raucous memorial after his death, calling him a "hunka hunka burnin' love." Some said he had the looks and bearing of a Shakespearean king.

John Charles Juliani was born in Montreal and raised in a working-class neighbourhood. He attended Loyola College and was an early graduate from the fledgling National Theatre School. He spent two seasons as an actor at Stratford before being hired as a theatre teacher at Simon Fraser University in 1966. The new university atop Burnaby Mountain east of Vancouver was a hotbed of radicalism in politics and the arts. Juliani bristled at an imposed curriculum and so infuriated the administration that he was banned from the campus in 1969.

Juliani was heavily influenced by the writing of Antonin Artaud, a Surrealist who championed a theatre based on the imagination. He long sought to erase the barrier between scripted text and sensory impression, between performer and audience, to mixed success.

After moving to the West Coast, Juliani launched a series of experiments in theatre. He credited these productions to Savage God, which was less a troupe in the traditional sense than a title granted to any performance involving Juliani. The name came from William Butler Yeats' awestruck reaction to Alfred Jarry's *Ubu Roi*: "After us, the Savage God?"

Savage God defied explanation, though many tried and even Juliani offered suggestions. Savage God was "an anthology of question marks," he once said. (It was, after all, the 1960s.) "Savage God is simply the Imagination," he told the *Vancouver Sun*, "insatiable, unrelenting, fiercely energetic, wary of categorization, fond of contradiction and inveterately iconoclastic."

In January 1970, Juliani married dancer Donna Wong, a ceremony conducted as a Savage God performance at the Vancouver Art Gallery. He repeated the process at the christening of his son. Wong-Juliani would be his domestic and drama partner for more than three decades.

In 1971, the streets of Vancouver were the scene of several spontaneous—and sometimes incomprehensible—performances under the aegis of PACET ("pilot alternative complement to existing theatre"). The $18,000 project, funded by the federal government, incorporated Gestalt therapy sessions in street performances. Theatrical events took place willy-nilly across the city, including malls, the airport, the library and Stanley Park. Admission was not charged, nor did all spectators appreciate their role as audience to avant-garde performance. A scene in which bicyclists wearing gas masks pedalled along city streets left many scratching their heads in puzzlement.

In 1974, Juliani moved to Toronto to set up a graduate theatre-studies program at York University. He called the program PEAK ("Performance, Example, Animation, Katharsis") and perhaps should have found a meaning for the acronym PEEK, as the instructor and his class stripped naked to protest against a lack of classroom space.

The challenge to the new Stratford artistic director in 1974 was written on a piece of parchment and delivered in London by Don Rubin, a York colleague. Alas, Rubin could not find a proper gauntlet and wound up ceremoniously striking Phillips with a red rubber glove, an absurd note to a theatrical protest.

In 1978, Juliani took the stage in a Toronto production of *Children of Night*, portraying Janusz Korczak, a doctor and teacher who ran an orphanage in the Warsaw ghetto. The critics were appalled. Gina Mallet of the *Toronto Star* said Juliani's performance sullied Dr. Korczak's memory. Jay Scott of the *Globe and Mail*, noting "the dreadfulness" of Juliani's acting, said the production robbed the dead of their dignity.

From the stage, Juliani challenged the *Star*'s critic to a public debate on the aesthetics of theatre. He also wrote a letter to the editor, noting that Holocaust survivors in the audience had wholeheartedly embraced the production.

Juliani wound up in Edmonton, where he continued to condemn the "exorbitance, elitism and museum theatre" of the establishment.

In 1982, he directed and co-wrote *Latitude 55°*, a feature film with just two characters—a slick woman from the city and a Polish potato farmer—set in a snowbound cabin. "It is filled with a passionate conviction that evaporates in pretentious pronouncements," the *Globe*'s Carole Corbeil wrote, "filled with truthful moments that evaporate in the desire to use every narcissistic trick in the book."

In a 1983 book examining the alternative theatre movement in Canada, author Renate Usmiani devoted most of a chapter to Juliani, a decision that got her a scathing rebuke from a reviewer who considered him worthy of little more than a footnote. "His works are curiosities; at best, they are worthy experiments in Artaudian theory," Boyd Neil wrote in a *Globe* review. "But they are neither popular . . . nor influential."

Juliani's years at CBC Radio in Vancouver were both productive and successful. Among the many projects he directed was a three-part adaptation of Margaret Laurence's *The Diviners*; *King Lear*, starring John Colicos; a thirteen-part series titled *Disaster! Acts of God or Acts of Man?*; and, famously, Ryga's *The Ecstasy of Rita Joe*, with Leonard George portraying a role once assumed on stage by his late father, Chief Dan George. The surprise selection of George was typical of Juliani's often brilliant casting.

Juliani directed a 1989 production of *The Glass Menagerie* at the Vancouver Playhouse with Jennifer Phipps and Morris Panych. *Globe* reviewer Liam Lacey praised a production that "opens up the play like an old treasure chest, and lets in some fresh air without rearranging or disturbing the work's original grandeurs and caprices."

Four years later, Juliani was directing a production of the mystery thriller *Sleepwalker* when actor Peter Haworth took sick shortly before opening night. The director suddenly found himself as the male lead. "Not even the most colossal egotist would want to do this," he said.

Dim Sum Diaries, a series of monologues written by Leiren-Young, received protests when aired by CBC Radio in 1991. One episode, entitled "The Sequoia," in which the white vendor of a luxury home delivers a tirade against the Hong Kong immigrant who cuts down two rare trees on the property, was accused of being racist. The playwright's well-intentioned exploration of stereotyping was charged with fostering those very prejudices.

After directing *Dim Sum Diaries*, Juliani urged the playwright to tackle an issue that was dividing his church. Leiren-Young remembers replying: "You're talking same-sex marriage in the Anglican Church and you want a straight Jewish guy to write this?" The resulting play, titled *Articles of Faith: The Battle of St. Alban's*, was staged at Christ Church Cathedral in downtown Vancouver to great acclaim. The collaborations between young playwright and veteran director succeeded in achieving Juliani's goal of inspiring dialogue through theatre.

Juliani had a reputation as a demanding taskmaster for novice and veteran actors alike. Rehearsals were jokingly called "Savage God boot camp."

He maintained a breakneck pace, both in the theatre and in the boardroom. He was artistic co-director of Opera Breve, a small company dedicated to nurturing young singers; president of the Union of BC Performers (ACTRA); and a former national president of the Directors Guild of Canada, among many boards on which he served.

Feeling fatigued in early August, Juliani was diagnosed with liver cancer. The end came swiftly. He died before the month ended.

For one who roused such passions, Juliani felt that he led a conservative life. "I have always been a square," he said.

A theatrical farewell to Juliani attracted hundreds to St.

Andrew's Wesley Church in Vancouver on Labour Day, a Monday and traditionally a quiet date on the theatre calendar. Those in attendance were encouraged to write remembrances on Post-It notes, which were then stuck to the church's pillars. The city of Vancouver declared the following March 24, which would have been Juliani's sixty-fourth birthday, to be Savage God Day.

October 11, 2003

INNOVATORS

Donald Hings stands in the backyard of his Burnaby home in 1988, leaning on the walkie-talkie he invented in 1937 while working for the Consolidated Mining & Smelting Company. PHOTO BY BILL KEAY, PROVIDED BY THE *VANCOUVER SUN*

Donald Hings

INVENTED WALKIE-TALKIE
(NOVEMBER 6, 1907—FEBRUARY 25, 2004)

Donald Hings was a self-taught electronics wizard whose modified two-way radio saved the lives of untold Allied soldiers in the Second World War.

Hings was credited as inventor of the walkie-talkie, although he himself never claimed the title. By nature a modest man, he preferred to describe his contribution as belonging to a natural evolution of advancements in the burgeoning electronics field.

Others were not as reticent to take credit. Motorola unveiled a portable radio in the early 1930s, although it needed to run off a motorcycle battery and only transmitted in Morse code. Some sources cite a team of US Army technicians at Monmouth, NJ. Toronto-born Al Gross claimed to have invented the two-way portable radio in 1938, although by then Hings's own radio was already in production.

An inveterate tinkerer, Hings was hired by Consolidated Mining & Smelting Company (now Teck Cominco). The company's geologists sought mineral deposits in isolated bush country, yet lacked a means of contacting civilization.

After much trial and error, in 1937 Hings developed a portable two-way voice radio for emergency transmissions. The radio was cased in a watertight container painted a bright yellow for quick recovery should a float plane sink. The radio was a marvel for bush pilots.

Further advancements came quickly, as such innovations as a speech scrambler, a noise filter, a voice magnifier and improved earphones made the technology ever more useful on battlefields. The Canadian military put his models through rigorous testing, including throwing a set over the edge of a seaside cliff. "By the time the army got through with them," Hings once said, "they had to be built like tanks."

The walkie-talkies designed by Hings and made available to Canadian and British troops in the Second World War were lighter, more durable and more powerful than any issued by friend or foe. For all his life, Hings would receive testimonials about the quality of his invention from grateful veterans.

The son of a decorated Boer War veteran who became a grower of fruit trees, Donald Lewes Hings was born at Leicester, England. His parents soon became estranged and the boy moved with his mother to Canada at age three. He was educated at grade schools in Lethbridge, Alberta, and North Vancouver, abandoning formal education to help support his mother, a bookkeeper. An inheritance of land brought them to Rossland.

The boy was obsessed by a new marvel of technology—the radio—and built his first crystal set at age fourteen. He helped establish the first radio station in the Kootenays and more than eight decades later would still be listed as a ham radio operator with the call sign VE7BH.

He worked as a labourer at a plywood plant before being hired by the mining company, an employer who indulged his insatiable curiosity.

In 1939, Hings travelled to Spokane, Washington, to file US patents on his portable two-way radio. After an exhausting day of lecturing a patent lawyer on the intricacies of electronics, a tired Hings was returning to his hotel room when interrupted by excited newsboys. Germany had invaded Poland. Canada would be at war within days.

The merits of his device in warfare were clear. After being seconded to the National Research Council, he was invited to Ottawa to demonstrate his equipment. He worked as a civilian with the Royal Canadian Corps of Signals, which would later name him an honorary colonel. The earliest examples were delivered to Britain shortly after the Dieppe Raid of 1942.

Hings called his wireless radio a "Packset." Motorola had developed what it called a "handie-talkie." A more familiar name is said to have been coined during a presentation to reporters in Toronto, when a soldier demonstrating the equipment was asked its purpose. "Well," the soldier said, "you can talk with it while you walk with it." Apocryphal or not, the device has ever since been known as the walkie-talkie.

A refrigerator factory in Toronto was retooled to manufacture the sets, about eighteen thousand of which were produced during the war. Most were designed for use in the European theatre, with its harsh winters, while others were modified for the tropics or use aboard a tank. The Canadian design was widely felt among the Allies to be the superior equipment. The sets lacked moving parts and were simple to operate, allowing soldiers in the field to share in their comrades' reconnaissance.

Although stories about two-way radios had appeared in newspapers even after the outbreak of war, the equipment was developed in an atmosphere of secrecy until a decision was made by the brass to unveil the wonder device.

A Toronto newspaper's headline captured the awe: "Miraculous walkie-talkie like quarterback to army." The newspaper reported, "To radio men it is a midget miracle, a tiny but tough combined broadcasting and receiving set, easier to operate than a hand-telephone set, light but tough enough for paratroopers to take along in aerial assaults on enemy airfields, versatile enough so, in combination, they become a military network of broadcasting and receiving stations for attacking troops.

"To infantrymen, the walkie-talkie is like giving a football team a quarterback."

For his service, Hings was made a Member of the Order of the British Empire in 1946.

After the war, he bought a parcel of land atop Capitol Hill in the Vancouver suburb of Burnaby. The spot, where he had camped as a Boy Scout, afforded an unobstructed view of neighbouring Vancouver and its harbour. Hings built a modest home for himself and his young family, surrounding it with towers, radar sheds, electronic shops and laboratories. Over time, he sold lots to his employees at cost, building a hilltop community of scientists.

His company, Electronic Laboratories of Canada Ltd., of which he was president and chief engineer, won many contracts from the Department of National Defence. Radar and antenna designs found application on the DEW (Distant Early Warning) Line across northern Canada.

Hings registered more than fifty patents, including some related to the thermionic vacuum tube and to a Doppler radar aircraft-landing system. Many involved airborne and subsea geomagnetic instruments for exploration of minerals. He even had a patent for an electronic piano.

The compound was a playground for innovative adults and curious children alike. "I thought every kid had a mad scientist as a grandfather," said Morgan Burke, the daughter of Hings's youngest daughter.

Hings retired in 1986. Although he had never attended a single university class, he was a member of the American Geophysical Union and the Association of Professional Engineers of BC.

A fall left him an invalid, as doctors feared his weakened heart could not withstand the stress of hip-replacement surgery. A rare excursion from his home came in 2001 when Governor General Adrienne Clarkson invested him as a member of the Order of Canada in a private ceremony in Vancouver.

April 7, 2004

STAN BRAKHAGE

AVANT-GARDE FILMMAKER
(JANUARY 14, 1933—MARCH 9, 2003)

Stan Brakhage, a leading figure in experimental cinema often described as a poet who used film instead of words, was regarded as a genius by cineastes.

His avant-garde works never played at the cineplex, yet his exploration of the boundaries of camera technique and editing structure influenced such directors as Martin Scorsese, Francis Coppola and Lloyd Kaufman, creator of the cult fave *The Toxic Avenger*. David Fincher, the director of *Seven*, was among his students, as were Matt Stone and Trey Parker of *South Park* infamy, in whose *Cannibal! The Musical* he appeared.

Many of his original techniques and images have been stolen over the years by advertisers and Hollywood. A hand-held camera, multiple exposures and films edited with jarringly quick cuts were all part of a pioneering approach radical in its time.

Brakhage did not merely expose film to light; in his hands, film was scratched, painted, burned and bleached. Once, too destitute to afford film, he sandwiched bits of flowers and moth wings between strips of Mylar splicing tape.

Brakhage made more than four hundred films, one a mere nine seconds long, while another lasted a fidget-inducing four hours and twenty-one minutes. Most were made without sound, which he felt spoiled the intensity of the visual experience.

"How many colours are there in a field of grass to the crawling baby unaware of 'Green?'" he asked in his 1963 book *Metaphors on Vision*. "How many rainbows can light create for the untutored eye? How aware of variations in heat waves can that eye be?"

His goal as a filmmaker was bold and presumptuous: "Imagine a world before the 'beginning was the word.'"

A Brakhage film often lacked narrative, a deliberate choice, which made his work inscrutable to many. A decade after his first film, *Interim*, produced as a nineteen-year-old in 1952, the *New York Times* at last reviewed one of his works, *Anticipation of the Night*, four years after it had been completed. The melancholy meditation on suicide, for which he even contemplated committing his own, did not impress the critic Eugene Archer, who wrote: "It might better be called 'Gleanings from the Cutting Room Floor.'"

Even those mainstream critics who admired his work were sometimes stretched for explanation. "There is beauty and serenity in Brakhage's world of constantly changing colors and shapes," Vincent Canby wrote in the *Times* in a 1975 review of *The Text of Light*. "Sometimes they fill the screen like volcanic eruptions; at other times they merely punctuate the black background, suggesting lazy, radioactive caterpillars looking for a rest."

Brakhage created meditations on subjects as mundane as domestic life and as sacred as sexuality. Many of his pieces were autobiographical. In 1959, Brakhage graphically documented the birth of one of his children in *Window Water Baby Moving*, filmed before camcorders became standard delivery-room accessories. At the time, television portrayed married couples sleeping in separate beds.

His best-known work is *Dog Star Man*, a series of shorts combined into a seventy-four-minute film released in 1964. The mythic themes of the watershed film have been compared with the poetry of William Blake. *Dog Star Man* is regarded as one of the greatest pieces of American cinema, although its audience has been substantially smaller than that for, say, *Titanic*.

"He was a painter or poet in cinema," said P. Adams Sitney, a film historian at Princeton University, "not a novelist like everybody else."

Sitney confidently predicts the filmmaker someday will be regarded as the pre-eminent artist of the twentieth century.

Brakhage was born in an orphanage in Kansas City, Missouri, where he spent the first weeks of his life named Robert Sanders before being adopted by Ludwig and Clara Brakhage. They named the boy James Stanley.

He attended high school in Denver and performed on the radio as a boy soprano. After suffering a nervous breakdown as a freshman at Dartmouth College, he dropped out and took up filmmaking. He met and was influenced by such figures of the avant-garde as Maya Deren and Kenneth Anger. The personal films of Marie Menken had a great influence on him, as did Jean Cocteau, the Italian neo-realists, and the writings of Gertrude Stein.

In 1957, he married Jane Collom, with whom he collaborated, and he would take as his subject their life together, as well as that of their five children.

Brakhage was a noted educator in filmmaking, lecturing at the School of the Art Institute of Chicago from 1969 to 1981 and teaching at universities in Colorado for more than forty years. He was also a prolific writer, although many of his essays were too dense for all but the most dedicated film student.

After divorcing in 1987, Brakhage moved from Lump Gulch to Boulder, Colorado. He later began a relationship with Marilyn Jull, whom he married in Toronto in 1989. They lived there for eight months, returning to Colorado only after he was unable to secure a suitable position at one of the universities in Ontario.

Among his many awards were Rockefeller and Guggenheim fellowships and, in 1986, the inaugural Maya Deren Award for independent film and video artists from the American Film Institute. When Brakhage became the first filmmaker to receive the prestigious Edward MacDowell medal in 1989, Scorsese presented the award in a ceremony at Peterborough, New Hampshire.

In 2002, Brakhage moved to Victoria, his wife's hometown, where he lived six months before dying of cancer. Though bedridden, Brakhage continued filming through the final days of his illness. He completed *Stan's Window*, which was filmed chiefly through the windows and doors of his sick room. He also scratched emulsion with his fingernail in his final work, titled *The Chinese Series*. Inspired by Chinese language and thought, it was incomplete at his death.

March 13, 2003

TRAILBLAZERS

Margaret Fane Rutledge

AVIATRIX

(APRIL 13, 1914—DECEMBER 2, 2004)

Margaret Fane Rutledge founded the famed Flying Seven, a legendary group of pioneer aviatrixes from Vancouver who showed a woman's place was in the cockpit.

Inspired by the wonders of flight after seeing an airplane aloft early in childhood, she became the first woman west of Toronto to earn a commercial pilot's licence. She was unable to earn a livelihood in the air, however, as even the smallest airlines refused to hire a woman pilot. She instead learned to operate a ham radio and is regarded as the first woman to do so for an airline in Canada, if not the world. Once in an airline's employ, she managed to pilot several commercial flights without mishap.

Margaret Rutledge was a stocky, square-jawed woman whose considerable aviation skills elevated her above every roadblock placed in her path.

Born in Edmonton at a time when newspapers cheered the "dizzy doings" of daredevils performing loops in rickety biplanes, she enjoyed a birthright as the daughter of parents thrilled by the dawning of the age of flight. Both her mother and father had flown as passengers in the first airplane to arrive in the Alberta capital.

Her father, who owned an automobile repair shop, later built a glider with his own hands.

Rutledge first flew aboard an aircraft in 1928. Three years later, a tour billed as the Trans-Canada Air Pageant landed in Edmonton. The thrilling display convinced the seventeen-year-old youth that her future was in the clouds. She scrimped for two years before enrolling at the Edmonton and Northern Alberta Aero Club, which had been launched with First World War ace Wop May as president and chief instructor. Rutledge became a prize pupil of Moss Burbridge, of whom it is said not one of his seven hundred students ever suffered an injury.

She trained on such biplanes as a Cirrus Moth, Gypsy Moth, American Eagle and Alexander Eaglerock, the latter a favourite of prairie barnstormers. On October 12, 1933, she was issued private pilot's licence No. 1317.

By doing the club's books and handling chores such as stretching fabric over the wooden ribs of an aircraft, Rutledge earned free flying time, according to aviation historian Shirley Render. The deal was a necessity for the ambitious pilot, whose earnings of $22 per week were not enough to cover lessons that cost $12 an hour. On August 29, 1935, she was issued commercial licence A1236, becoming the first woman in Western Canada to be so qualified.

As the twenty-one-year-old woman prepared to join her family in moving to Vancouver later that year, the male members of the club presented her with an engraved watch acknowledging her achievement. Pleased to discover six other licensed women pilots in Vancouver, Rutledge travelled to Burbank, California, to meet Lauretta Schimmoler, a pilot from Ohio and one of the founders of the Ninety-Nines. The group, which took its name from the ninety-nine licensed women pilots who attended its inaugural meeting, decided Canada had too few pilots to permit a chapter. The journey was not an entire bust for Rutledge, however, as she did get to meet the famed Amelia Earhart.

Rejected in the United States, Rutledge returned to Vancouver determined to organize her own informal club. The Flying Seven, formed on October 15, 1936, captured the imagination of Vancouver by staging a dawn-to-dusk flight the following month. A Golden Eagle and a pair each of Fleets, Fairchilds and Gypsy Moths took twenty-five-minute spins in the air, a member taking off as another landed. The stunt began precisely at 6:59 a.m. when Tosca Trasolini took off without a hitch despite drizzle and a dangerous ground fog at Sea Island Airport, today the site of Vancouver International Airport.

Over time, the Flying Seven adopted a smart-looking uniform of culottes with a silk blouse worn beneath a wool jacket, topped by a distinguished Glengarry hat, all in grey.

After the outbreak of war, some of the women were rebuffed in their attempt to join the Royal Canadian Air Force as pilots or instructors. Instead, they appealed for "dimes or dollars to buy our boys more planes" as part of a Vancouver Air Supremacy Drive.

On a sunny midweek day in June 1940, the Flying Seven staged a "bomphlet" raid over the city, dropping a hundred thousand "Smash the Nazis" pamphlets. As it was, a brisk southeast wind, combined with a city ordinance forbidding flight lower than 3,000 feet, swept many of the handbills into the waters of English Bay and Burrard Inlet.

Shortly before the outbreak of war, Rutledge's skill won her a small measure of fame. Ginger Coote hired her to handle reservations and operate the radio for his Bridge River & Cariboo Airways. She was posted to Zeballos, an isolated gold-mining town on the west coast of Vancouver Island where she was one of three unmarried women in a rambunctious town otherwise populated by fifteen hundred miners.

Grant McConachie, who owned Yukon Southern Air Transport, and on whose recommendation Rutledge had been hired, had a flare for publicity. He leaked word of the unusual job and its circumstances. Newspapers across the continent ran an article on her duties, some including a photograph portraying the no-nonsense operator posed in front of a large console. A believe-it-or-not headline in the *Chicago Daily Tribune* was typical: "Canadian woman pilot is operating a radio station."

"I was supposed to be the radio operator but I also dispatched, did the waybills for the freight, tied up and fueled aircraft, and herded loggers and miners on and off the planes," she once told Render, the aviation historian. "I took a dunking more than once while trying to push a drunk logger onto a plane."

She described her reservation duties as simply counting the number wishing to leave. If three or fewer, she ordered the airline's Waco to Zeballos. If ten or fewer, she called for the Norseman, although a full load meant the seats would be removed and passengers would sit atop their luggage.

Coote sometimes allowed her to take control of the aircraft, making her the province's only woman working as a commercial pilot. While he had confidence in her abilities, he had other motives. "I remember the day we went to Gun Lake to put in a radio station," Rutledge told Render. "He told me to fly the Norseman while he went back to read the newspaper. When we got there I called him back to take over as I had never landed it by myself. He was sound asleep and too groggy to wake up—he liked his liquor. When we docked he fell off the float and I had to jump in after him." She rescued him only with difficulty, as his breeches had filled with water.

In Zeballos, Rutledge would leave gold bullion worth one million dollars on a chair overnight in the airlines' unlocked office.

"Nobody thought anything about leaving that stuff around loose," she told historian Jack Schofield, "but you'd never leave a case of whisky unattended."

In addition to Coote's Waco and Norseman, Rutledge also flew Barkley-Grows owned by Yukon Southern. In fact, when McConachie invited her to join him in the cockpit on a test flight of a Lockheed 14 passenger plane from Vancouver to Edmonton, it would be her final flight as a pilot.

Coote's bush company was one of ten gobbled up to form Canadian Pacific Airlines in 1941. Rutledge returned to Vancouver where she would enjoy a twenty-year career, during which she became superintendent of reservations.

In retirement, she lectured about the Flying Seven and offered her memories to a succession of aviation historians. After marriage, she made her home within sight of the jets taking off and landing at the much-expanded airport where she had once taken part in the dusk-to-dawn flight.

January 5, 2005

Gertrude Ettershank Guerin
[Klaw-Law-We-Leth]

CHIEF

(MARCH 26, 1917—JANUARY 25, 1998)

Delbert Guerin once asked his mother why the family always ate at a restaurant called the New Pier on Main Street in Vancouver. She told him that, fifty years before, the Guerins had been hustled to a corner table at the Trocadero Grill on West Hastings Street. The manager explained, "Indian people want to be in here, they have to sit in the corner out of sight." The family walked out, never to return.

Gertie Guerin did not take such snubs lightly. She traced her lineage to the great warrior Ke'epalano, who defended his people against raids by the Haida. Gertie, too, was a warrior, her weapon of choice her character.

A daughter of the Squamish on her mother's side and of the English on her father's, she was left at age twelve to care for a younger sister, Vivian, when their mother died. Life was harsh on the reserve. Even as Vancouver's skyline began to grow across the harbour, the Squamish trudged from their homes to the single tap that provided water for the entire reserve.

As a teenager, Gertie Ettershank worked at a cannery, where she met a quiet, hard-working, slick-haired fisherman. Victor Guerin was ten years older, a handsome lacrosse player. In 1936, they were married at St. Paul's, the reserve's church where Gertie had been christened and confirmed.

Delbert was born in 1938, an eleven-and-a-half-pound baby whose birth left Gertie bedridden for years. Other children followed—Beverley, Beryl, Glenn and Darryl. In 1953, the brood moved to Victor's home reserve of Musqueam, on the north arm of the Fraser River on the southwestern edge of Vancouver. Victor worked as a longshoreman outside the fishing seasons. Gertie dreamed of greater things for her children, pulling them out of residential school, where several grades studied in a single classroom, and sending them to the local public school.

She joined the PTA. "It took two years there before the members would notice me but when I didn't disappear they just had to say 'hello,'" she recalled. She was appointed to the social committee. "This meant I got to do the dishes after most social events. But I didn't mind. I asked some of the members to help and they did and then we were friends." She became PTA president.

In 1959, at forty-two, Guerin was elected to a two-year term as Musqueam chief and is believed to have been the first Native woman in Canada elected to such a post. She made it mandatory that adults perform acts of community service—painting, cleaning, home repairs—before they were issued welfare. Beryl Guerin recalled, "She used to say, 'We need self-esteem. We need to feel that we are important to ourselves.'"

When she left office in 1961, Musqueam had its first running water, city garbage pickup, new dikes and paved roads. A city dump planned for the riverfront was stopped. Guerin fought the city for the right of the Musqueam to vote. Hers was the first name registered.

After her term as chief, she helped found the indispensable Vancouver Indian Friendship Centre and the Vancouver Native Police Liaison Society. She had setbacks, such as her defeat for school board on a reformist slate in 1968. In 1970, Victor Guerin was struck by a huge pipe while working on the waterfront. His back was cracked, his hip smashed and his left arm severed above the elbow.

Delbert followed his mother as chief, and while he held that office he lent his name to the famous suit—*Guerin v. The Queen*—that won the reserve a $10-million judgment against the Crown for leasing nearly sixty-six hectares of reserve land to the Shaughnessy Golf Club. He gave the credit to his mother: "The Guerin case came about because of me listening to her complain, no doubt about it."

A fighter to the last, Gertie Guerin received the last sacrament of the Roman Catholic Church four times. On her final night, she told her hospital roommate: "I'm getting tired. I think it's time to go."

She was buried beside Victor, who died in 1989, in the reserve cemetery, a short stroll from the golf course. At St. Michael the Archangel, the reserve's tiny wooden mission church, Rev. John Horgan has mounted an icon of St. Gertrude the Great (1256–1302), a Benedictine mystic known for her writings and leadership. Below is a plaque in honour of Gertrude Guerin—the saintly and the secular honoured together. Father Horgan celebrated her funeral mass in the reserve's gymnasium, so great was the turnout.

April 2, 1998

Dr. Josephine Mallek

DOCTOR

(JULY 4, 1912—JULY 24, 2004)

Josephine Mallek was the first woman doctor on the staff at St. Paul's Hospital in Vancouver and a mentor to younger doctors wrestling with the demands of family and practice.

Dr. Mallek enjoyed a unique perspective on her profession and its effect on family life. She was the spouse of a doctor, the mother of a doctor, and the daughter of doctors.

After more than a half-century as a practising physician, she became a tireless advocate for seniors, lobbying for adequate medical care and buttonholing politicians to demand funding for affordable housing. She also revived a moribund Vancouver Medical Association and, as its president at the age of seventy-eight, took on Social Credit premier Bill Vander Zalm in a fee dispute with doctors. "Unless the government pulls up its socks," she warned, "it may be reduced to a paragraph in the history books." The Socreds were trounced in an election the following year.

Born the second daughter to immigrant doctors in Montreal, Josephine Schacher would later describe her childhood as having been spent in a waiting room. The family lived in a three-storey granite townhouse on East Sherbrooke Street with her father's

The daughter of doctors, by age eight Josephine Mallek operated the sterilizer and set out dressings for her parents' medical office on the ground floor of the family home. She gained a medical degree despite the university's quotas on both women and Jews. She later became the first woman doctor at St. Paul's Hospital in Vancouver. PHOTO COURTESY OF PROVIDENCE HEALTH CARE ARCHIVES medical office on the ground floor. By age eight, Josephine was responsible for operating the sterilizer and setting out dressings.

Her father, Nathan, was an immigrant from Austria who studied medicine at Cornell University in Ithaca, New York. After moving to Montreal, he needed to learn French and ended up marrying his language tutor, Sophie Puchovsky, a Ukrainian emigrée who had earned a medical degree in France. They found in Canada a refuge from the persecutions suffered by Jews in Europe.

Josephine spoke Yiddish to her grandmother, English to her parents, and French to her playmates.

A favourite game at home was playing school, with her older sister repeating the lessons she had learned that day. By the time Josephine entered Grade 1, she could read, write and do basic math. She skipped two grades in elementary school before entering Baron Byng High School, where landscape painter Anne Savage was the art teacher and the student body included such future notables as poet A.M. Klein.

Schacher won a scholarship to McGill University, completing a medical degree in 1936, followed by a master's degree in endocrinology in 1938. At the time, the school maintained quotas both on the number of Jews and on women admitted to medicine—twenty-nine in 1938, only 6.3 percent of the class.

In 1938, she married ophthalmologist Howard Mallek, whom she had met while returning a microscope to a fraternity house.

They completed their residencies in wartime England, where Howard tried to enlist shortly after the Dunkirk evacuation. He was turned down, told the only work likely for a doctor in that stage of the war was in treating German prisoners of war.

The couple endured a perilous crossing of the Atlantic at a time of U-boat attacks. They settled in Vancouver, opening adjacent medical offices in the Birk's Building, a terra-cotta landmark at the downtown's main intersection. They would later move to the nearby Vancouver Block, maintaining neighbouring offices for forty-five years.

With an expertise in such fields as diabetes, growth-hormone problems and adrenal-gland collapse, Dr. Mallek joined her husband on the staff at St. Paul's. The hospital was founded and administered by the Sisters of Charity of Providence, a Roman Catholic order, many of whose members became her patients.

Over the years, aspiring young women asked Mallek for insight on the difficulties of juggling a medical career with family life. She assured them that it was a possibility and became a mentor to many. Her own children remember spending weekend mornings in the car with a packed picnic lunch, waiting for their mother to complete house calls.

In 1987, Dr. Mallek ended her practice after fifty-one years, although she was far from ready to retire. She became president of the Vancouver Medical Association, reviving the organization through the simple but effective tactic of billing doctors for membership. She knew that in many medical offices harried doctors unhesitatingly signed cheques for invoices gathered by their assistants.

In 1990, a fee dispute between the BC Medical Association, of which the Vancouver association is an affiliate, and the provincial government saw Mallek, a noted raconteur, provide scathing criticism. She told reporters that she was especially angry at the premier and his finance minister for meddling in matters about which they knew little.

"I can't imagine the premier taking out an appendix or [Mel] Couvelier doing a colectomy," she told the *Vancouver Sun*. "Let's not forget each role—[we] are the health-givers and the government's role is the insurance business."

Mallek also warned the Socred government not to underestimate the doctors' influence at the polls. "Each one of us has developed a following of hundreds of people who we've worked hard to look after and to get their trust ... and we're not going to do anything to lose that trust." The doctors were seen as having won the dispute over a new fee schedule after months of protracted negotiations, demonstrations, work-study sessions and service withdrawals.

Looking back on her career in a 1996 interview, Mallek bemoaned the profound change in the administration of medicine.

"I practised during the golden age when it was an honoured profession," she told newspaper columnist Nadine Jones. "If I wanted to spend a whole morning with a patient, I did. I'm too much of an individualist to comply with today's rules.

"Doctors today have to think of how much they are costing the system, whether they are ordering too many tests, or whether they could be sued for negligence for not ordering enough tests. If they are 5 percent off the pattern of practice, they have to account for it. It's all politics and money."

In recent years, she served on many boards and city committees responsible for examining seniors housing and health care.

Dr. Mallek suffered a stroke while storytelling during a dinner party. She was taken to St. Paul's, the hospital whose corridors she had walked for so many years. Six days later, on July 24, 2004, she died in her sleep.

July 31, 2004

Douglas Jung was the first Chinese Canadian to be elected to Parliament—a surprise considering so few Vancouver voters shared either his political views or his ethnic heritage. Here he rides the streets of Vancouver as a Progressive Conservative candidate during the 1958 campaign. PROVINCE NEWSPAPER PHOTO, PROVIDED BY THE VANCOUVER PUBLIC LIBRARY, 41609

Douglas Jung

LAWYER, MEMBER OF PARLIAMENT
(FEBRUARY 25, 1924—JANUARY 4, 2002)

|D| ouglas Jung was elected to the House of Commons ten years after Canadians of Chinese ancestry were belatedly awarded the franchise. His triumph was the more remarkable in that few voters in Vancouver Centre had shared his Progressive Conservative sympathies in recent elections. Fewer still shared his ethnic heritage.

Every advance in Jung's career seems to have been a marker in the history of race relations in Canada. He was the first Chinese Canadian to be accepted to the British Columbia bar; the first to appear before the BC Court of Appeal, the highest court in the province; the first to be elected to Parliament; and the first to represent Canada at the United Nations.

He was a trailblazer in the land of his birth, a man of sharp intellect and ambition who came of age just as Canadian society began to dismantle legally sanctioned racism.

In 1944, when his own country considered him to be less than a full citizen, Jung risked his life by volunteering for duty as a saboteur behind Japanese lines.

As a veteran, he at last earned the right to vote. After his election, he campaigned to redress some of the wrongs committed against fellow Chinese Canadians.

Douglas Jung was born in Victoria. His father, Vick Ching Jung, an immigrant of humble means from Guangdong Province in China, named him after Douglas Street, the city's main thoroughfare. He was the youngest of three sons.

His birth came eight months after the implementation of the Chinese Immigration (Exclusion) Act on July 1, 1923, which essentially closed Canada's doors. The date came to be known as "Humiliation Day" in the Chinatown ghettos.

He inherited a world in which property covenants forbade him from buying land in many neighbourhoods. He was barred from the practice of pharmacy, medicine and the law. He would sit in segregated movie houses. He also could not swim at Crystal Gardens pool, the glass-topped oasis that was a playground for Victoria's other children.

Jung completed his public-school education at Victoria High School as the Second World War raged. He enlisted soon after the Canadian government reversed a policy barring Chinese Canadians from serving in the armed forces.

The British wanted to recruit soldiers of Chinese ancestry who could be sent into Asian jungles to blend in with the local population as secret agents.

Jung volunteered for clandestine warfare and was sent to isolated Commando Bay near Penticton for intense training in the arts of demolition, sabotage and silent killing. "We looked like cutthroats," Jung recalls in *Unwanted Soldiers*, a 1999 National Film Board documentary. "We were not in military uniforms. We were unshaven, disheveled." Jung, a sergeant, belonged to Force 136 of the British-led Special Operations Executive. His perilous assignment was to organize resistance behind Japanese lines. He was equipped with a suicide pill, which was to be used to avoid torture should he be cornered. As a spy, capture meant death.

"We were prepared to lay ourselves down for nothing," Jung said. "There was no guarantee that the Canadian government was going to give us the full rights of Canadian citizenship. We were taking a gamble."

Both of his brothers also served. Arthur Jung piloted a Lancaster on bombing missions over occupied Europe, while Ross Jung served in a medical unit. The war ended not long after Douglas Jung parachuted into the Borneo jungle.

He returned to British Columbia in 1946, taking advantage of veterans' benefits to complete a bachelor of arts and a law degree at the University of British Columbia.

In 1947, the provincial government ended restrictions on voting for Chinese Canadians. That same year, the federal government revoked its discriminatory immigration laws, although it would be another two decades before any large-scale immigration from Asia would be permitted.

Jung, who continued to serve in the militia as a captain, began practice as a lawyer after graduating in 1953. He was a dapper man, rarely seen without a tie and jacket, his black hair carefully groomed and precisely parted on the left side.

He made his electoral debut as a Conservative candidate in a provincial by-election held on January 9, 1956. Leslie Peterson, a future cabinet minister, handily won Vancouver Centre for Social Credit. Jung finished a respectable second, a moral victory that also had a touch of the historic. His candidacy was the first by a Chinese Canadian for a seat in any Canadian legislature.

Just seventeen months later, he became a Member of Parliament in a shocking upset. Ralph Campney, a veteran of the First World War, was defence minister in the Liberal government and thought to be safe in the federal riding of Vancouver Centre. His challenger was a thirty-three-year-old upstart in a riding that had only about fourteen hundred Chinese Canadian residents.

Jung polled 9,087 votes to Campney's 5,357. "The Giant Killer," as he was called, helped John Diefenbaker to form a minority government. Jung said he had become a Conservative because he could never support a party that had discriminated against his people. The 1958 *Canadian Parliamentary Guide* notes tersely: "First M.P. of Chinese extraction."

He won re-election by a massive 10,117 votes in the Diefenbaker landslide of 1958. That same year he was elected national president of the youth wing of his party.

Jung caused a stir when he said he wanted to visit China, which had fallen under Communist control. The issue was controversial in the Chinese-Canadian community, which he once described as his best ally and his harshest critic.

As an MP, Jung proved to be indefatigable advocate. He convinced the government to grant an amnesty to those Chinese who came to Canada under false names. He also helped to create the National Productivity Council, now known as the Economic Council of Canada.

Jung lost his seat in 1962 to Liberal J.R. Nicholson, an industrialist who was a pillar of the establishment and would later serve as BC Lieutenant-Governor. The Conservative also lost elections in 1963 and 1965, before bowing out as a candidate.

Jung ran a successful legal practice specializing in immigration issues for many years.

He liked to tell a story about his debut as Canada's representative to the Legal Committee of the United Nations, an appointment made by Diefenbaker. "I took my place there," Jung later told the *Vancouver Sun*, "and an usher came over and said, 'I'm sorry, sir, but this seat is for the Canadian delegation.'" Jung replied, "I am the Canadian delegation."

February 2, 2002

WARRIORS

PATRICK DALZEL-JOB

MODEL FOR JAMES BOND

(JUNE 1, 1913—OCTOBER 12, 2003)

So daring were his wartime escapades, so thrilling his adventures, Patrick Dalzel-Job was called a real-life James Bond.

Dalzel-Job was a charismatic commando who later settled in the bush country of the British Columbia Interior and whose derring-do was every bit as exciting as that of Ian Fleming's fictional spy. In fact, Fleming was his possible inspiration's commander in a cloak-and-dagger unit that operated behind enemy lines in occupied Europe.

Whatever Dalzel-Job's unintentional contributions to the genre of spy thrillers, the British officer is remembered in Norway as a hero. He disobeyed direct orders from superior officers and risked court-martial by evacuating the fishing port of Narvik. Hours later, German bombers flattened the centre of town.

Like his fictional counterpart, he had disrespect for authority in general and for foolish commands in particular. He spoke several languages, admired gadgetry and enjoyed tinkering with explosives. He also had Scots blood, of course. However, unlike James Bond, he was not a drinking man, nor did he display an appetite for carnal variety. "I only ever loved one woman," Dalzel-Job once confessed.

Dalzel-Job was the son of a military officer and the father of another. He was born in London, the only child of Capt. Ernest Dalzel-Job and the former Ethel Griffiths. His father, who commanded a machine-gun company, was killed in action during the Battle of the Somme on July 11, 1916.

The boy was a sickly child, often stricken with fever. After some schooling at Berkhamsted in Hertfordshire, he was moved by his mother to Switzerland when he was fourteen. The alpine climate improved his health. Never one for sports before, he became an expert downhill and cross-country skier.

The years in a village in a landlocked country only fed his wanderlust. As a young man, he purchased a sixteen-ton topsail schooner, which he named *Mary Fortune*. With his mother as sole crew, he sailed across the North Sea to Norway, whose fjords and channels he would explore as far north as the Soviet border. In an initiative reminiscent of Erskine Childers' adventure novel *The Riddle of the Sands*, in which the hero surveyed the German coast before the First World War, Dalzel-Job sent detailed navigational reports back to the Admiralty.

The winter of 1938 was spent at Tromso, a port north of the Arctic Circle where he befriended a timber merchant and his family of ten children. The eighth among them, a thirteen-year-old girl named Bjorg Bangsund, was invited to join the mother in the galley for the remainder of the journey.

On the outbreak of war in September 1939, Dalzel-Job returned to Tromso to deliver Bjorg to her family. When he went to bed that night on the boat, he found a brief love letter written on a scrap of paper tucked beneath his pillow.

He abandoned the schooner and rushed home by commercial line to volunteer with the Royal Navy.

Dalzel-Job was charged with helping to organize the Allied expeditionary force landings in Norway. He was not only familiar with Norway's treacherous coastal waters but also had a working knowledge of fishermen dialects.

His brilliant scheme was to use local fishing boats. The

diesel-powered *skoyter*, as the Norwegians called them, were dubbed puffers by Dalzel-Job, a name that appears in the official records. The ruse fooled German bombers. More than fifteen thousand soldiers and four thousand civilian refugees were transported during a two-month campaign without the loss of a single life at sea.

That tremendous success was followed by an even more memorable accomplishment. After a German force was chased from the fishing port of Narvik, Dalzel-Job, a lowly sub-lieutenant, organized a withdrawal of the civilian population against the explicit orders of his superiors. The entire town of forty-five hundred was evacuated in a single day. Dalzel-Job "smiled to the children, was courteous to the mothers, and cursed the skippers on board and any people on the quay who were not quick to help," Narvik mayor Theodor Broch said.

As Dalzel-Job expected, the Germans bombed the port. The buildings were made of wood and the explosions sparked a fire that levelled the town centre. Only three civilians died in the bombing. "It seemed a miracle," Dalzel-Job said. "I think I succeeded because I had the trust of the skippers and because the movements were made to look like fishing trips."

He expected to face a court-martial for his disobedience, a threat removed only after King Haakon VII sent his personal thanks to the British Admiralty. Later, the grateful monarch presented the young officer with the Knight's Cross of the Royal Norwegian Order of St. Olaf (First Class).

The Norwegian campaign was a military fiasco for the Allies, as the expeditionary force soon fled and Neville Chamberlain resigned as British prime minister. However, the Norwegian merchant marine carried Allied supplies throughout the war, while the rescue of the royal family forged a bond between the conquered land and Britain.

Dalzel-Job continued harassing the enemy in Norway, taking part in raids by motor torpedo boat. He reported on German shipping movements from a lonely secret post atop the summit of Atleo, an island. He also provided an intelligence briefing for an unsuccessful attack on the dry dock at Bergen by four midget submarines in 1943.

After being taught to parachute by Lloyd Adams, a lieutenant from Toronto who would be killed in action on D-day, Dalzel-Job was assigned to the 30th Commando Assault Unit, under Ian Fleming's command. The unit worked ahead of the Allied front line, slipping behind enemy defences on risky reconnaissance and intelligence-gathering missions. On one such patrol late in the war, Dalzel-Job, who had been promoted to lieutenant commander, accepted the surrender of the German port city of Bremen from the acting burgomaster at city hall. With Bondsian panache, he then proceeded to capture the valuable and well-guarded shipyard, including two destroyers and sixteen of the latest submarines, without firing a shot.

After V-E Day, he returned to Norway to seek out Bjorg Bangsund. "At nineteen, she was taller, of course, than the child I had left, and her hair was longer and lighter; but she had the same enormous blue eyes under finely arched eyebrows, and the same white, even teeth, with a space between the two top ones in front," he wrote.

They were married in Oslo on June 26, 1945, six years after she had left behind a love note in her schoolgirl hand. They lived briefly at Onich, near Fort William, in Scotland, where a son was born in 1946.

Dalzel-Job longed to return to sea and his carefree mariner's life of prewar days. The *Mary Fortune* had been lost in Norway after being seized by the Germans and sold to a collaborator. Since wood was in short supply in Europe after the war, Dalzel-Job moved to Newfoundland, where he ordered a schooner to be built. Alas, the boat builder went bankrupt.

He then drove his family across Canada by truck. They settled west of Prince George in the Francois Lake area near Burns Lake, where they lived in a log cabin on 160 hectares of what was mostly untouched bush. He later joined the Canadian navy and was stationed at Esquimalt, near Victoria.

The couple returned to England in 1956, and then to Scotland in 1960, transforming a barren moor into a spectacular garden at Nead an Eoin, on the rugged shore of Loch Carron. Dalzel-Job taught math, chemistry, English and nautical sciences at the local school.

His beloved Bjorg died of cancer in 1986 and, in his grief, Dalzel-Job at last completed his memoirs. He had sold magazine articles as a youth and likely would have enjoyed a literary career had war not intervened. His crackerjack autobiography, titled *From Arctic Snow to Dust of Normandy*, received favourable reviews on its publication in 1991. Among the book's fans were the Queen Mother and actor Roger Moore, one of the cinematic Bonds.

The pain of his loss was expressed in the book's dedication: "To the memory of a blue-eyed little girl from the Arctic."

Dalzel-Job died at his home in Plockton. He was left a son, retired major Iain Dalzel-Job, of Rosyth, Fife, a one-time classmate of Prince Charles at Gordonstoun and commander of a leading company of Scots Guards in the bayonet assault on Mount Tumbledown in 1982 during the Falklands War.

The news of Dalzel-Job's death renewed the parlour game of naming the model for cinema's best-known spy.

The evidence on Dalzel-Job's behalf is compelling: He was a master on skis and could ski backward (*On Her Majesty's Secret Service*); manned a midget submarine (*For Your Eyes Only*); nearly died in a headfirst plunge after his parachute became tangled (*Moonraker*); blew up enemy warships (*The Spy Who Loved Me*); and, as a commando, had a licence to kill. His identity number was not 007, however, but the less lyrical 036652.

"We all recognized Patrick immediately the first novels came out," said Peter Jemmett, a Royal Marine who belonged to the commando unit. "He carried off things almost every day that would have got anyone else killed."

Other candidates with a claim as the inspiration for Bond include war hero Fitzroy Maclean; spy boss Wilfred Dunderdale, known as Biffy; Russian-born secret agent Sidney Reilly; and, not the least, Fleming's older brother, Peter.

Dalzel-Job once quietly admitted that Fleming had told him that he was the model for his secret agent.

Unlike millions of others, Dalzel-Job never once watched a Bond film. "When you have led such an exciting life," he said, "you don't need to see a fictional account of it."

November 8, 2003

ROY BORTHWICK

DESTROYED BRIDGE OVER THE RIVER KWAI
(JULY 28, 1920—OCTOBER 15, 2007)

Roy Borthwick piloted the bomber that destroyed a bridge known to moviegoers as the famous span in the movie *The Bridge on the River Kwai*. At the time of the 1945 attack, the Vancouver pilot and his crew had no inkling their dangerous mission would one day become one of the more renowned incidents of the Second World War.

Borthwick, an RCAF flight lieutenant, was based with the Royal Air Force's No. 159 Squadron near Calcutta, India. Many Canadians served in the crews for the B-24 Liberators at the Allied base, and he had logged more than two thousand hours flying time on a variety of missions. Many of these involved long round trips amounting to more than 4,800 kilometres, including a successful mine-laying operation off the coast of Malaysia.

An attack on shipping at Satahib Bay in Thailand led to a risky assignment for the pilot. His unenviable task was to distract the defenders while other crews bombed and strafed vessels in the bay. Not only did he manage to draw fire from anti-aircraft artillery on the ground, he scored a direct hit on a 3,000-ton depot ship, which, set ablaze, soon sank.

Daring and brave though these escapades were, it would be his

The son of a Vancouver grocer, air-force pilot Roy Borthwick destroyed a bridge over a river in Thailand. The attack would later become familiar to moviegoers as The Bridge on the River Kwai. *Borthwick enjoyed the popular film, though its story of Allies blowing up a bridge constructed by prisoners of war was entirely fictional.*
PHOTO COURTESY OF SUSAN BORTHWICK

role in an attack on a bridge over a Thai river that would bring re-porters and historians in search of his insights many years after the war.

On June 24, 1945, Borthwick piloted one of eleven bombers sent on an all-day mission to bomb the bridge at Kanchanaburi, a station on an important supply link known as the Death Railway. The Japanese occupiers had compelled native workers and Allied prisoners of war to complete a Bangkok-to-Rangoon route through the jungle. Many thousands of these slave labourers died under ap-palling conditions and unspeakable torments.

Borthwick had developed a technique to avoid fire from the heavy machine guns likely to be found at either end of a bridge, he told James Elliott of the *Hamilton Spectator* in 1998. "Instead of climbing up and away from the bridge after the bomb had gone, I would dive down and hug the ground, about thirty feet or so, have my nose gunner hose the area right in front of us for maybe three or four minutes, then climb up to one thousand feet and come down again."

The pilot succeeded in making five passes along the river, each time dropping a thousand-pound bomb. The bombs smacked into the muddy water before exploding eleven seconds later. One of them, likely the first, destroyed a span of the steel-and-concrete railway bridge.

Only many years later did the mission and, especially, the target become entrenched in the popular imagination thanks to a novel written by a Frenchman. Pierre Boulle had been the overseer of a Malaysian rubber plantation when war broke out, after which he worked as a secret agent organizing resistance to the Japanese. He was captured by the Vichy French while trying to escape by floating along the Mekong River on a makeshift raft, and spent a year in prison.

After the war, he wrote several stories, novels and memoirs about his wartime escapades, the most famous being *The Bridge Over the River Kwai*, published in 1954. The movie, which had the slightly different title, *The Bridge on the River Kwai*, was released three years later. Starring William Holden and Alec Guinness and directed by David Lean, it was a huge hit at the box office and won seven Oscars.

Borthwick was entertained by the movie, but somewhat disappointed in the retelling, his widow said recently. The captivating story of PoWs building the bridge only to have it destroyed by Allied commandos was entirely fictitious.

While he emerged unscathed in the attack on the Kwai bridge, Borthwick had a close call after a low-level attack on another railway bridge near Three Pagoda Pass, south of Moulmein. He was pulling up after dropping his payload when one of the crew delivered an urgent message.

"Skipper, we've been hit in No. 3 [engine] and we've got black smoke pouring from it," the flight engineer reported.

The engine seized and burst into flame. Attempts to extinguish the blaze failed.

"Now, our only option was to ditch, and this is not good news," Borthwick wrote in a memoir published online by the British Columbia chapter of the Burma Star Association. "Very few Liberator ditchings were successful, as they had a tendency to break up badly when they hit the water. The soft bomb-bay doors would collapse, water hitting the aft bulkhead with such force it would break the back of the aircraft.

"Since we had no alternative and the fire was threatening to break into the wing, then to the gas tanks, we prepared for ditching. The rest of the crew moved onto the flight deck and [I was secured] to my seat and backrest with the Sutton harness so I wouldn't go through the instrument panel when we hit the water.

"When we were down to fifty feet above the water, I began easing off the throttles to just above stalling speed. At twenty feet, ready to cut the throttles, I saw out of the corner of my eye no flames."

The pilot rammed on more power. Low on fuel, he decided to land on a small dirt strip on Akyab, a small island in the Bay of Bengal from which the Japanese had retreated. He landed the bomber with great skill, the nose of the plane coming to a stop against the jungle foliage at the far end of the runway. A British Army officer soon arrived by jeep with a present of a bottle of Scotch. Somehow, the bomber had missed several bomb craters left by a recent enemy attack.

Shortly after war's end, Borthwick was awarded the Distinguished Flying Cross for displaying "cool judgment, courage and great devotion to duty."

Roy McIntosh Borthwick's father was a Scottish émigré who opened a grocery in Vancouver with Oliver Killick. Their B&K Economy Stores would grow to become a citywide chain. At Christmas, young Roy accompanied his father in delivering food hampers to needy families. He competed on the rugby pitch and in the swimming pool for Magee High School.

With an older brother in the navy, he decided to enlist in the Royal Canadian Air Force. He joined up in 1941 and, after undergoing initial training at Edmonton, took his first flights at Lethbridge, Alberta, before graduating to twin-engine Ansons at Fort McLeod, Alberta. One of his instructors had been a Hollywood stunt pilot, teaching an eager pupil some tricks, which he would find handy in evading enemy fire.

Keen to get overseas, the pilot instead spent another two years on Prince Edward Island before being returned to the West Coast to train on Liberators at Boundary Bay airport south of Vancouver. He was then ordered to Montreal, where he was to receive a new Liberator to be flown to North Africa and on to Asia. The planes, as it turned out, were not yet ready and he sailed instead by troop ship from Halifax to Greenock and then from Southampton to Bombay.

After the war, he sought a pilot's job with Trans-Canada Airlines. Unfortunately, his application went astray and many other demobilized flyers had generated a lengthy queue by the time it was found. The opportunity had slipped away, so he instead became a marketing manager for the family's grocery stores.

Borthwick later worked as a manager with a heavy-equipment company involved in major road-building projects commissioned by the province's Social Credit government.

In 1947, he married June Turkington, whom he had known years before. Nicknamed "Lari" (pronounced Larry), she had picked up the moniker at boarding school (on Saturdays, the girls paired off at dances, the taller ones instructed to lead, a role for which they teasingly earned boy names). After the war, he was reunited with her and a romance was kindled on the North Shore ski slopes that overlook the city.

He spent his fiftieth birthday on the Pacific as a deckhand aboard a yacht skippered by his friend John Dunfield in the biannual Victoria-to-Maui race.

November 8, 2007

WILLIAM ALLISTER

POW, ARTIST

(OCTOBER 5, 1919—NOVEMBER 2, 2008)

An actor, artist, novelist, filmmaker and scriptwriter, William Allister's creative impulses were stifled but not extinguished during forty-four months of wartime mistreatment by Japanese captors.

Imprisonment demanded painstaking ingenuity. A pilfered swatch of canvas, a paintbrush improvised from a whittled stick and shoe-brush bristles, and a smear of crankcase oil secreted from a Japanese truck were the materials that allowed him to create surreptitious paintings of his Hong Kong concentration camp.

Camp overlords were known by nicknames, some hinting at their particular cruelties: "Piston Fists," "Little Napoleon," the "Kamloops Kid." The latter was a notorious tormentor whose childhood experience of racism in British Columbia had left him with a dark heart and evil intent.

Allister suffered much deprivation and several beatings. Once, a Japanese officer unsheathed a sword, threatening to cut his head off. Allister's defiant riposte—"Tell him my boss doesn't want his men working without their heads"—was deliberately ignored by a fellow prisoner serving as translator, likely saving his life. The brutal treatment brewed a hatred that still simmered more than three

Though he spent nearly four years as a prisoner of war in the hands of the Japanese, William Allister lived a life dedicated to art. With actor, artist, novelist, filmmaker and scriptwriter all on his resume, here he is in his studio, doing one of the things he loved best. PHOTO COURTESY OF MONA ALLISTER decades after his release. Memories of punishments endured and friends lost to treatable diseases could not be erased.

"Starvation, beatings, illness, insults, psychological wounds," he wrote in a memoir. "Hostility and anger ran deep in my blood."

In 1983, the impulse to resolve these feelings lured him to the Japanese shipyard where he had been forced to labour in appalling conditions. During a month-long visit, he immersed himself in the culture of a people he had come to loathe but in whom he eventually found much to praise. A son of one of the camp guards spent a week as a guide in Tokyo. At a precise moment, as a ceremonial dancer removed one kimono after another, Allister felt his animosity evaporate.

The journey unlocked a vision of how he could reconcile a simmering hostility with a newfound admiration. "As an artist, I would paint toward peace, paint as I'd never painted before, stretching to the limits, soaring, exploring new forms, new harmonies," he wrote. "Visions of giant canvases marrying East and West unfolded before me."

Remarkable for their bright colours and expression of an exuberant spirit, his works can be found in collections around the world. He had more than thirty one-man gallery shows.

This transformation became the subject of a 1995 Canadian documentary film. *The Art of Compassion* offers parallel portraits of the artist and a Japanese-Canadian architect who had been interned during the Second World War. Both men found inspiration from their experiences.

Allister detailed his own imprisonment in *Where Life and Death Hold Hands*, a 1989 memoir remarkable for recapturing the stifling life of prison camp in which the veneer of civilization has been all but stripped away.

"Forget—no. But forgive—yes, if forgiving could encompass disapproval. To really understand was to forgive, to grasp the nature of the illness, the historic path of the virus in the bloodstream of a nation," he wrote. "Open the gates of war anywhere, and hellish monsters roam the earth."

Born to Ukrainian Jewish immigrants in the small Manitoba village of Benito on the Saskatchewan border, he grew up in Montreal, where he graduated from Baron Byng High School.

In April 1939, he won a regional acting award at the Dominion Drama Festival. He portrayed a shell-shocked veteran in the one-act play *Road of Poplars*. He could not have known his own promising life would be consumed by another dreadful war in a few months.

Having "tasted the sweetness of early recognition," as he put it, the young actor joined a touring repertory company, performing zany comedies for audiences in the Catskills resort area of New York. The Village Vanguard club in Greenwich Village offered a venue for satirical sketches. With steady stage work and having had performances aired on the CBC radio network, Allister pursued advanced studies in drama in New York.

In 1941, he abandoned his classes to return home to enlist in the Royal Canadian Corps of Signals, undergoing basic training at Huntington, Quebec, and Debert, Nova Scotia. An arduous regimen left him capable of transmitting eight words per minute in Morse code, a woefully slow rate.

He sailed to Asia aboard the liner SS *Awatea* after volunteering for a mission in which he joined other raw recruits in bolstering the British garrison at Hong Kong. The thrill of so exotic a posting, where the brazenness of the gambling and prostitution shocked even a Montrealer, was soon lost when the Japanese attacked on December 8, 1941.

He found himself in the heat of battle. Surrounded, he fired his rifle. "A figure was dead centre in my sights . . . silhouetted against the sky as I pulled the trigger. He dropped. The thought vaguely registered that I had just killed a man. And so easily."

He compared the experience to a duck-shooting booth at a country fair.

He was soon taken prisoner. Other comrades chose suicide over surrender. In retrospect, it might have been the wiser decision. The PoWs began to waste from a starvation diet and the subsequent diseases that thinned the ranks—dysentery, diphtheria, beriberi, cholera. Beatings were common, and delivered on whims so as to be almost unpredictable. The prisoners bravely expressed their outrage through vulgar though dangerous stunts, the most notorious of which involved urinating into a teapot used by a man they called "Little Napoleon."

Meanwhile, back at home, the Allister family in Montreal endured a year of waiting before learning the fate of their son. Eventually, he received a letter.

"I opened the letter with trembling fingers and stared uncomprehendingly at the first sentence: 'We were overjoyed to know you are a prisoner of war.' Overjoyed! There I sat—in shit up to the eyeballs, half dead, crawling with lice, exhausted, starved, disease ridden, jolted by electric feet, a bloody walking skeleton—and they were overjoyed? Had they all gone balmy? It took a while to see it their way."

In January 1943, about seven hundred prisoners were ordered into the hold of a rusty freighter. The men used buckets as latrines, ate rancid rice and got only scant seconds of fresh air on deck in the four-day journey to Japan. They were to be slave labourers at the Nippon Kokan Shipyards at Kawasaki.

On arrival, the men filled out forms detailing their civilian employment. The wily Allister listed librarian and painter. The translation of the latter placed him "on a thin plank suspended over the Pacific Ocean, painting the side of a ship." His true calling eventually became known to his captors, one of whom established Allister in a stockroom with a supply of fresh paints and canvases. Happy to be painting and not eager to return to the deadening monotony of meaningless work, Allister painted with deliberation, calling on his showman's instincts to turn his procrastination into a performance.

The ruse ended when the would-be patron realized the painting depicted the prisoners as kindly and their jailers as fiends. The canvas was smashed to the ground and the painter ordered back onto the scaffolding.

In March 1945, he was moved to another camp that was "decrepit, small, uninviting, in a coal yard on the outskirts of Tokyo beside a rail ramp."

Allister learned of the end of the war with the Emperor's radio announcement of surrender. Six days passed before an Allied aircraft flew overhead. The prisoners cheered, waving bed sheets while using mirrors to reflect sunlight. The pilot dipped his wings in acknowledgment. Allister remembered it as "the most magnificent symbolic salute ever received."

The memoir offers an unsparing account of his own behaviour in those lawless days, as he joined colleagues in search of prostitutes. They entered a factory staffed by women workers, most of whom fled in fear. Allister confronted one woman but when she pushed past him he did nothing to restrain her. He returned to camp, having contemplated, though not committed, a crime. In his favour, he saved three young Japanese guards from being executed by a trigger-happy American soldier.

After returning home, he moved to Los Angeles in 1946 to pursue an acting career suspended by the war. He took bit parts in such movies as *Berlin Express* and *Joe Palooka in the Big Fight*. He did not stay long, finding "the jungle values of Hollywood were lower than the jungle values of prison camp."

He turned to writing and painting, earning a living as a commercial artist and scriptwriter in New York. He composed a first draft of a novel in a Brooklyn graveyard, a rare place of solitude for a budding author with a young family—he had married a model from Ottawa—in a rumbling metropolis. A stint as an executive for a Montreal advertising agency financed a decade of revisions.

The completed book, *A Handful of Rice*, published in London by Secker & Warburg in 1961, describes the tribulations of Canadian prisoners captured at Hong Kong. The novel, which won a minor literary prize, was translated into Dutch and Norwegian.

Allister moved his family to San Miguel de Allende in 1962, seeking in Mexico to explore an abstract style. He proved to be prolific and his works popular, he once told the author John Virtue, generating jealousy among more established painters, though he himself did not think much of his own efforts.

"They weren't too good, but they were all different, experimental.

'This is the kind of stuff we've been looking for,' people told me. Unfortunately, I outsold all the pros, the seasoned artists and teachers."

While in Mexico, he completed a second novel, *Time to Unmask the Clowns*, which went unpublished. He returned to Canada before the decade ended, writing film scripts and radio plays, as well as documentaries. In 1986, he won an Author's Award from the Foundation for the Advancement of Canadian Letters. He settled in Delta, where he was active in the Hong Kong Veterans Commemorative Association.

The return journey to Japan resulted in the publication of his vivid memoir in 1989. *Where Life and Death Hold Hands* won a prize for the promotion of intercultural relations. The memoir was translated into Japanese in 2001.

His paintings received wide praise. "Striking from across the room, Allister's canvases first appear to be sizzling Zen calligraphy," Robert Amos, a painter and art critic for the *Victoria Times Colonist*, wrote of a 2003 show. "As you approach nearer, his free play with colour kicks in. Up close, you'll find a wealth of narrative and illustrative detail worked into the imagery."

A successful showing took place at the Canadian Embassy in Tokyo, a building designed by Raymond Moriyama, the architect featured in the documentary with Allister.

Several of Allister's prison camp paintings survived the war, most of which are destined for the Canadian War Museum in Ottawa. Two other works, one depicting a Japanese sentry and the other a ship sunk in Hong Kong harbour, were sewn inside the pant leg of John Burton, a fellow prisoner from Toronto. A daughter took ownership after his death. They now hang on the living-room wall of her home in Prince Edward Island, a silent reminder of beauty amidst despair.

November 29, 2008

Syd Thomson

OFFICER

(NOVEMBER 14, 1914—NOVEMBER 8, 2008)

The Battle of Ortona would be known over the years by other names—Bloody Christmas, or Italy's Stalingrad. In December 1943, Canadian troops faced the unenviable task of evicting battle-hardened German soldiers from the Adriatic port.

The battle reduced the ancient city to rubble as warriors fought street by street, house by house, room by room. It was in this ferocious hand-to-hand combat that the Canadians developed a technique called mouse-holing, in which they attacked an adjacent house by blowing a hole in shared walls.

The costs were heavy for the Loyal Edmonton Regiment and the Seaforth Highlanders of Canada, the latter commanded by Syd Thomson.

The dawning of Christmas morning brought no peace, nor any respite from the fighting. As men continued to do battle, Thomson and an imaginative quartermaster prepared a Christmas dinner so memorable the survivors gathered every year after the war to mark the meal.

Thomson retired from the military as a brigadier-general with medals to his name and a vicious scar in one leg, which he would show his children at their request if they were on good behaviour.

Sydney Wilford Thomson was born in Salmon Arm in British Columbia's Shuswap region to Cyril and Eva (née Bromham) Thomson. His Scottish-born father co-owned a garage and later became a dealer of General Motors cars and trucks. Cyril Thomson was elected mayor of the municipality in 1928, serving in the post for fourteen years.

Syd Thomson dropped out of school in Grade 10 to earn money for the family as the ravages of the Depression began to be felt. He picked apples in the summer, worked in a grocery store, and unloaded and delivered the contents of a freight car of coal, which he would always describe as the most arduous job of his life.

In the 1930s, he joined the local company of the Rocky Mountain Rangers, needing his father's consent because he was underage. He trained as a signaller, and was a lieutenant in the company when Germany invaded Poland on September 1, 1939. Britain declared war two days later. On September 9, Thomson received orders to mobilize the company. Canada declared war the following day.

He was ordered overseas in 1940, by which time he had transferred to the Seaforth Highlanders, arriving at the height of the Battle of Britain. He served as a platoon commander under Maj. Cecil Merritt, the Vancouver officer who would win a Victoria Cross for his bravery at Dieppe.

While stationed in the south of England, officers were invited to take tea at Streat Place, a Sussex estate boasting a Jacobean manor house. The teetotal hospitality not being appreciated by the officers, they drew straws to determine attendance. Thomson picked a short straw. As it turned out, he met a young woman who would become his wife after the end of the war. He would later offer detailed descriptions of his first glimpse of the host's eighteen-year-old daughter, Catriona Bromley-Martin, who wore a blue dress while standing against a magnificent fireplace. Had the officers more fully appreciated the deprivations to be faced in the coming months of war, they might not have been so reluctant to take part in the tea.

In June 1943, the Seaforth Highlanders set sail for the Mediterranean aboard the *Circassia*. They joined in the invasion of the island of Sicily the following month, the beginning of a long and bloody Italian campaign. By now a captain, Thomson served as a company commander.

Three days after the invasion, the company stumbled across a makeshift roadblock. Italian soldiers opened fire, shooting the captain through the thigh of his right leg. The medical officer gave the commander an injection of painkillers, after which he was placed in the manger of a barn, his sidearm removed by comrades for safekeeping.

He awoke to find he was sharing the manger with two peasants carrying pitchforks. He reached for his gun only to discover he was unarmed, according to the official regimental history by Reginald Roy. To his relief, the farmers sought only hay for their oxen.

Sent to Sousse, Tunisia, to recuperate, he was treated with an experimental wonder drug, penicillin, and was soon back in the field.

In October, he led his men in an advance across a rocky knoll near a heavily defended hill. A company slipped across without incident, but the enemy pinned Thomson's soldiers with artillery, mortar and machine-gun fire. A smokescreen failed to offer cover and four enemy tanks appeared on the right flank. The battalion had yet to face such intense enemy fire.

Thomson, by now an acting major, led his men in an assault that called for an advance across an open, muddy area as long as ten football fields. The Seaforths charged uphill while facing the afternoon sun to capture Hill 1007 (Monte San Marco). Their commander was awarded the Military Cross for his "cool and skillful leadership," which "was an inspiration to his men throughout."

The Seaforths continued the slow fight northward. Their war took a different turn at Ortona, which was part of a general advance by the Eighth Army up the Italian Adriatic Coast. General Bernard Montgomery, denied Rome by indomitable German defenders, lighted on Ortona as an alternative target that promised to distract the press and cause them to forget his promises to take the Italian capital by Christmas.

The 1st Canadian Division, which included Thomson's Seaforths, was ordered to take the town. The cramped port offered little room to manoeuvre. Crack German paratroopers defended the ancient town, building roadblocks with engineers to force the attacking Canadians into the few open squares, which were ringed by machine-gun nests to create a killing ground.

Battling in close quarters, the Edmontons and Seaforths fought a slow, bloody battle in the waning days of 1943. On the morning of Christmas Eve, the Germans launched a dangerous counterattack, which, at such close quarters, eliminated the use not only of the Canadians' artillery but even mortars.

The regimental history offers a crisp description of events that day: "The threat was such that acting lieutenant-colonel Thomson made his way to the company positions and, although constantly exposed to sniper, machine-gun and mortar fire, remained with the forward troops, directing and co-ordinating the defence, and showing a cheerfulness and coolness under fire which did much for the men beating off the attack," Roy wrote in his 1969 history, *The Seaforth Highlanders of Canada, 1919–1965.* "To see the commanding officer of the battalion at such a time somehow gave confidence to the private soldier, and Thomson's unruffled calm and big smile acted like a tonic."

The Canadians held their positions before returning to the dangerous task of claiming streets one house at a time. Thomson would be awarded the Distinguished Service Order for his action in the battle.

Christmas Day dawned, promising nothing more than another full day of stiff fighting. However, Capt. D.B. Cameron, an enterprising quartermaster, scrounged linen, candles and chinaware from the ruined homes of Ortona on which to serve a holiday meal. Tables were arranged in rows behind the thick walls of the church of Santa Maria di Costantinopoli. The companies ate in relays. The pipe major blew his pipes and a signals officer played the church's harmonium, even as shells whistled and exploded outside. The padre led volunteers in singing "Silent Night," as well as jauntier carols.

"Soup, roast pork, vegetables and Christmas pudding, along with a bottle of beer for each of the tattered, scruffy, war-weary soldiers was served," Thomson recalled many years later. The menu also included cauliflower, apple sauce, mashed potatoes with gravy, and even mince pie.

Dirty plates were stacked on the altar, while a side altar was covered by boxes of fruit and canned food.

"Between December 20 and the 28th, we lost forty-two killed and seventy-eight wounded," Thomson said. "Christmas in Ortona—the meal—yes. But the spirit of the occasion, the look on the faces of those exhausted, gutsy men on entering the church is with me today and will live forever."

After a week of vicious street fighting, the Germans finally withdrew, leaving farewell notes that promised renewed battle in the next fold of hills to the north.

By the time the last shot was fired and the last mopping-up patrol had returned, 1,372 Canadian soldiers had been killed during the battle.

After taking part in the fight to break the Gothic Line in 1944, Thomson returned to England as an acting colonel to command the Canadian Infantry Training Unit at Aldershot. He reverted to lieutenant-colonel to take command of the Black Watch in the Netherlands, where he was mentioned in dispatches.

After the war, he returned to the Shuswap, where he went into business with his friend "Big" Jim Stone, a much-decorated Seaforths officer. The men built a resort at Salmon Arm named Sandy Point. Thomson followed his father by running a General Motors dealership. He also owned an interest in the local bowling alley.

In 1950, Thomson rejoined the Canadian army, serving with the United Nations Observers Group in Pakistan. He spent months wandering the disputed Himalayan border region, covering the valleys by jeep and the foothills by mule and pony. "These two armies, Indian and Pakistan, under tough physical conditions, have been facing one another for five long years," he wrote to Stone, who, in turn, would go on to distinguished service in the Korean War. "Daily they sharpen their knives, clean their weapons and scowl across the line."

On his return to Canada, Thomson became an executive with Hiram Walker & Sons, rising through the distillery's ranks until becoming European sales manager in 1964. While in London, he became a director of the United Rum Merchants Ltd., as well as a trustee of a fund for Canadian veterans.

He returned to Canada on his retirement in 1977, building his own home north of Victoria, and sailed to the nearby Gulf Islands to explore anchorages. He also built greenhouses, even coaxing tobacco plants and tropical fruits from Vancouver Island's temperate climate.

In May 1987, he returned to Italy, where he offered an eyewitness account of the fight at the Gothic Line for a battlefield study conducted by the Canadian Land Forces Command and Staff College of Kingston, Ontario.

Thomson returned to his Salmon Arm birthplace in 1996, eventually living in a cottage next door to his eldest daughter. From there, he looked out on Sandy Point. His ashes were cast upon Shuswap Lake.

January 1, 2009

Jim Stone rose in rank from private to regimental commander in the Canadian army during the Second World War. This picture, taken of Stone in 1951, shows him after he returned to combat duty in Korea, during which his tactics and leadership helped outnumbered Canadian troops repel a furious Chinese assault at Kap'yong.

PHOTO BY PAUL E. TOMELIN, PROVIDED BY THE CANADA DEPT. OF NATIONAL DEFENCE FONDS/LIBRARY AND ARCHIVES CANADA, PA 128846

Jim Stone

SOLDIER

(AUGUST 2, 1908—NOVEMBER 24, 2005)

Big Jim Stone was a soldier's soldier. Gruff in manner, disciplined by nature, domineering in person, he was thought arrogant by some, yet his bravery was unquestioned. He once greeted news of an enemy assault by barking, "Let the bastards come!"

Stone rose from the rank of private to command a regiment during the Second World War, fighting in Sicily and northward on the Italian peninsula to bloody Ortona and beyond. He returned to action in the Korean War, his tactics and the bravery of the men under his command halting a fearsome Chinese advance at Kap'yong.

He was one of only twenty-two officers in the Canadian army ever to be awarded the Distinguished Service Order (DSO) three times. He also had a Military Cross to his credit.

A physically imposing man—bald, with ropy muscles in thick arms, and a brush moustache—his features were more than once likened to those of an eagle, a comparison he did not care for. To incur his displeasure was dangerous. Stone was as fierce a disciplinarian as he was a warrior.

James Riley Stone, who was born in Gloucestershire, trained as a cadet in England before immigrating to Canada in 1927. He was working in a forestry camp in Alberta's Peace River district when word reached him of the outbreak of war in Europe. He rode his horse out of camp on the first leg of a four-day trek to Grande Prairie, where the eager six-foot-five soldier joined the Edmonton Regiment as a thirty-one-year-old private.

By the time the Eddies fought across Sicily and onto the Italian boot, Stone had risen up the ranks to become a company commander. On the outskirts of Ortona, a picturesque Tuscan seaside town, German snipers plagued the Canadians, who eventually found an undefended trench along which they managed to sneak beneath the guns and into town.

The major was "resourceful, independent-minded, determined, brave to the point of near recklessness," according to the popular military historian Mark Zuehlke. Stone would need all those qualities to survive the grim battle for the ancient town. He devised a bold strike at the heart of the German defence with tanks charging into the centre of the town with the support of the infantry. The ruse caught the enemy by surprise, but just as the daring tactic seemed about to succeed, the lead tank stopped for fear of mines. According to Zuehlke's riveting account in *Ortona*, the major jumped aboard the tank only to hear the tank commander balk at risking his $20,000 machine.

"I've got twenty to thirty men here with no goddamned armour at all and they're worth a million dollars apiece," Stone yelled at the tank commander. "You're just a bunch of goddamned armoured sissies."

Just then, a German antitank gun began firing on the row of tanks. Stone threw a smoke grenade and raced headlong toward the gun. He lobbed a fragmentation grenade before seeking cover against the enemy gun's steel shield, silencing the gunners on the other side. The Canadians eventually captured the ruined town at great cost.

Later, Stone chafed at being the second in command. When he asked for a transfer, his commander refused, insisting that Stone "was the Edmonton Regiment."

After his bravery at San Fortunato Ridge, in which he led an antitank platoon into the midst of German defences, the major was awarded a DSO. He was promoted to lieutenant-colonel and in 1944 at last took command of the Loyal Edmonton, as the regiment had since become known. He saw further action in northwest Europe, earning a bar to the DSO, and was preparing for a tour in Asia when the Japanese surrendered.

After the war, he ran a hotel in Salmon Arm, where he settled into a domestic life with his wife and the first of several children. He maintained a military connection as commander of the Rocky Mountain Rangers.

He returned to combat duty with the outbreak of the Korean War as commanding officer of the 2nd Battalion, Princess Patricia's Canadian Light Infantry. Soon after arriving by troopship at Pusan in December 1950, Stone was told his men were to be sent as reserves near the front line. With the memory still fresh of the 1941 debacle at Hong Kong, when green Canadian troops became inevitable casualties of a Japanese assault, the commanding officer insisted his men had come to Korea to complete their training before facing the enemy. He even visited US Lt.-Gen. Walton Walker to press for a guarantee. Not wanting a political battle with the Canadian government, the commanding general agreed. (He would die in a traffic accident later that month.)

The training time also afforded Stone a chance to weed out those whom he saw unfit for battle. "Much 'scruff' that was hastily recruited has now been returned to Canada," he wrote. "Troops here are fit, morale high, show lots of guts in close contact."

He would later contend that he had not removed all the misfits after some men died drinking canned heat (methyl alcohol). According to author John Melady, the troops were ordered to march past the corpses as a lesson.

On their way to the front, the Canadians came across a massacre of American soldiers who had hunkered down for the night in a deserted hamlet only to be killed as they slept. Many were still in their sleeping bags. Stone ordered the Canadians be outfitted only with a single blanket each. They might be uncomfortable, he reasoned, but they would not end up with throats slit.

Sleep would be an impossibility in the battle for which he and his men will be remembered.

A massive Chinese assault had left troops from the Republic of Korea in a disorganized retreat. Stone, who had only days earlier returned after suffering from smallpox, was ordered to defend one side of a river valley atop Hill 677. He did a reconnaissance from what would soon be the enemy's assaulting point, determining the likely strategy for the Chinese attack. His recce and his experience fighting the Germans in the hills of Tuscany would prove invaluable on the night of April 24, 1951.

The Chinese attacked in great strength, vastly outnumbering the Canadian defenders, who were somewhat unnerved by their stealth—the Chinese travelled silently, rubber footwear muffling noise until the moment when a piercing whistle or bugle call signalled the start of an attack. The startling noise heralded the start of a bloody battle, the Pats raining murderous machine-gun fire on the Chinese, who had the disadvantage of climbing a steep hill.

Still, their overwhelming numbers came close to overrunning Canadian positions. The fighting in close quarters was fierce and desperate. A platoon leader bravely called for artillery strikes on his own position, trusting his men's slit trenches would protect them from the aerial assault. At times, the outcome looked dicey. A captain asked to pull back, but Stone refused. "I told him to stay there, that nobody could pull out, if we ever lose that hill, we lose it all," he said.

In the morning, Stone ordered an air drop to an isolated platoon, which had exhausted its supplies, including ammunition. The Americans unloaded their cargo with pinpoint accuracy to the relief of the Canadians below.

The attack was repulsed. The Chinese had died by the dozens, if not hundreds. The losses to Big Jim Stone's Patricias: ten killed, twenty-three wounded. "Kap'yong was not a great battle, as battles go," he would write many years later. "Personally I believe that

Kap'yong was the limit of the planned offensive of the Chinese at that time."

Stone was convinced his men would have been annihilated had the Chinese pressed on. Still, the defence of Hill 677 undoubtedly saved many United Nations soldiers, who won time to reorganize following their hasty retreat.

In any case, the Pats were awarded a United States Presidential Unit Citation, a rare honour. Stone received a second bar to his DSO.

After Korea, he qualified as a parachutist as the 2nd Princess Pats joined an airborne brigade group called the Mobile Striking Force. In 1953, he became chief instructor at the Royal Canadian School of Infantry at Camp Borden in Ontario. Promoted to colonel the following year, he was appointed provost-marshal of the Canadian Army. He was seconded to the federal justice department in 1958 and later served as senior deputy commander of penitentiaries.

In 1957, he founded the Military Police Fund for Blind Children, raising money for recreational activities and medical equipment. His own daughter, Moira, known as Plumsy, had lost both eyes to cancer. While attending a school for the blind at Brantford, Ontario, the girl had asked her father to treat classmates who could not afford candies at the school's canteen. Stone was heartbroken and angered by the lack of resources and founded the fund the year after the death of his daughter in 1956, aged seven.

He was named a member of the Order of Canada in 1994 for his charitable work, not his heroics. He considered the fund for children his greatest accomplishment. He died at The Lodge at Broadmead in the Victoria suburb of Saanich, aged ninety-seven.

December 27, 2005

Hugh McDonald, a brilliant scholar, worked as a seaman in the merchant marine, as shown here in a photograph taken aboard ship, circa 1937. He enlisted soon after the attack on Pearl Harbor. After the war, he helped smuggle Jewish refugees into Palestine before being captured by the British, who imprisoned him on Cyprus. He eventually settled in British Columbia, where he donated his spectacular collection of rare renaissance books to the library at Simon Fraser University. PHOTO COURTESY OF DAVID MCDONALD

HUGH McDONALD

CLASSICS SCHOLAR

(JULY 20, 1920—JULY 22, 2001)

A simple conversation with Hugh McDonald often turned into a learned discourse. He could speak with an engaging confidence on such diverse topics as ancient Athenian economics, Gregorian chants, sixteenth-century Venetian printing, and, from personal experience, the founding of modern Israel.

The bare outline of his life captures his diverse and contradictory interests. He was born to Irish immigrants and became a scholar of classics; a man of words who fought fascism as a paratrooper; a Gentile who volunteered to help refugees build a Jewish homeland in Palestine; a Wall Street financier who built and lost his own brokerage house; a dedicated book collector who overcame a bibliophile's natural possessiveness to transfer a unique Renaissance collection to a university library.

Hugh McDonald was born in San Francisco "in a world that didn't have radio, much less television or the computer," he once told me. "So we read." He devoured the adventure stories of Frank Merriwell and Tom Swift, but the path of his life was blazed when Jesuit teachers introduced him to the classics in high school. "Classical Greek and Old Testament Hebrew fell into place before I could even find out that they were difficult," he said.

A brilliant student blessed with a knack for language as well as a photographic memory, McDonald graduated from Stanford University. He was a tall, rawboned recruit when he enlisted with the US Army within days of the attack on Pearl Harbor. He was trained as a paratrooper, although his family is uncertain as to his complete combat record.

After the war, he entered Harvard Law School. One day, he and roommate Harold Katz attended a meeting about the plight of Jewish refugees. Soon after, the two men dropped out of school to join Aliyah Bet, the clandestine movement of immigrants into British Mandate Palestine.

McDonald and Katz served aboard the *Hatikvah*, a rusty, Canadian-built cutter that had been an icebreaker on the St. Lawrence River. During the war, the US Coast Guard used it for anti-submarine patrols. *Hatikvah*, which is Hebrew for "hope," as well as the name of the Jewish national hymn, had 1,442 Polish, German, Romanian and Hungarian refugees on board as it made a surreptitious journey from the Italian Riviera across the Mediterranean Sea.

The passengers—Holocaust survivors—spent the daytime in terrible conditions below deck so as not to be spotted by British patrols. Two babies were born at sea, but hopes for a future in Palestine seemed doomed when a British cruiser and a pair of destroyers converged on the cutter just as the shoreline of the passengers' promised land came into sight.

British marines boarded the *Hatikvah*, using stun grenades and tear gas to subdue the crew and angry passengers. The boat was towed into Haifa harbour under the cover of darkness on May 17, 1947. All aboard the *Hatikvah* were imprisoned for illegally entering Palestine.

The *Palestine Post* noted that the funnel bore a Star of David and the words "Eretz [The Land] 1947," as well as a green shamrock and the words "Eire 1922." The latter decoration was McDonald's work.

"Hugh was thumbing his nose at the British," said Katz.

McDonald was deported to an internment camp on Cyprus, spending several weeks behind barbed wire.

The Haganah, the underground Jewish military force, enlisted McDonald, Katz and others to sneak a bomb aboard a British ship. The action was to be in retaliation for the British seizure of *Exodus 1947*, whose passengers were returned to France.

First, though, McDonald had to break out of the internment camp to pick up explosives from Haganah agents on Cyprus. He did so successfully, but on sneaking back into camp was spotted by a sentry, who opened fire. McDonald escaped injury and rejoined his comrades without being identified.

The British allowed 750 refugees to enter Palestine each month from a list provided by Jewish organizations. The Haganah used its influence to have McDonald and the other plotters added to the list.

The British unwittingly loaded members of the plot aboard the *Empire Lifeguard*, the same prison ship that had transported them to Cyprus. One of the men boarded the ship with a pronounced limp—a pencil-sized detonator had been secreted in his anus. The conspirators assembled a bomb while aboard. The ship arrived at Haifa on July 23. While the men waited on the docks to be processed, a dull boom heralded the success of their mission. The *Empire Lifeguard* sank slowly in the harbour. No lives were lost in the sabotage and the plotters eluded authorities.

During his time in Palestine, McDonald vowed—should he be lucky enough to survive—to name his first daughter after the beauty of Lake Kinneret (Sea of Galilee).

After returning from the Middle East, he took post-graduate studies in classics, economics and law at Harvard. He then moved to New York City, where he began a career as an economist in 1951. He was a broker, a venture capitalist and a merchant banker in a career that took him to Chicago, Denver, and, in 1965, Vancouver. He retired in 1988 and moved to Victoria.

Through his many moves, McDonald remained a dedicated bibliophile, haunting bookshops around the globe in search of treasures.

While on leave in London in 1943, McDonald said, he had visited one memorably run-down bookstore. "I went inside," he recalled years later, "found a marvelous quantum of old Greek books, and a clerk who seemed to know Greek almost as well as I did. I bought a battered copy of Xenephon's complete works and had it shipped home." After the war, an acquaintance noted that McDonald's book had been published in the early years of the sixteenth century by Aldus Manutius, the great Venetian Renaissance printer.

"I'd had an Aldine volume on my shelves for three years before I knew it was an Aldine," he said. "I add, parenthetically and hopelessly, that the beat-up little shop in London was Bernard Quaritch, perhaps the greatest rare bookstore of the past 200 years. The clerk was from Oxford and may have been the Regius Professor of Greek. I tiptoe now when I enter the place."

In 1996, McDonald's collection of 106 Aldine volumes was acquired by the W.A.C. Bennett Library at Simon Fraser University in Burnaby. The books were bought with a donation made by businessman Morris Wosk, an old friend with whom McDonald had worked on campaigns to sell Israeli bonds. The collection was valued at $500,000 at the time and included a first edition of Plutarch, the Greek biographer and philosopher, worth $25,000. McDonald was a voracious reader who was said to have read all fifteen thousand volumes in his enviable library.

A year before his death, McDonald was one of several non-Jewish volunteers to be honoured with a certificate of appreciation from the government of Israel at a ceremony in Las Vegas.

McDonald retained a most nimble mind even as his health began to fail. He was teaching himself Aramaic, the ancient Syrian language, at the time of his death. He died in his sleep during a morning nap two days after his eighty-first birthday. Among his survivors was a daughter, known as Kini, whose formal name is Kinneret.

September 4, 2001

LAWMAN

ROBERT McDOWELL

MOUNTIE PURSUED MAD TRAPPER
(AUGUST 18, 1908—FEBRUARY 20, 2003)

In 1932, Const. Robert McDowell joined a party of twenty-one Mounties, trappers and Natives who tracked a desperate gunman across the frozen tundra of the Northwest Territories. The pursuit of the Mad Trapper of Rat River, who went by the name Albert Johnson, lasted for weeks in minus-forty weather, the hunt gripping radio listeners and newspaper readers in the grim winter months of a Depression year.

Two men were dead and two others grievously wounded by the time the dramatic manhunt ended on a frozen river in the Yukon. McDowell is believed to have been the last living witness to events that inspired several books and a Hollywood movie.

The Mounties called the famous case the Arctic Circle War, though their enemy was a lone killer. To the chagrin of police, the desperado became a folk hero to some people, who found in his beef with authority an echo of their own frustrations in a time of deprivation. The uncertainty of the trapper's identity even after so many years has only added to the allure of what transpired in that frigid hinterland.

It all began on a minor matter. A complaint by Gwich'in, also known as Loucheux, trappers about traplines being tampered with led the RCMP to send Const. Alfred (Buns) King and Special Const. Joseph Bernard to call on a stranger who had built a log cabin in a clearing near the banks of the Rat River. When the trapper refused to open his door, the pair returned to Aklavik.

A search warrant was issued and two more were added to the party—Special Const. Lazarus Sittichinli and Const. Robert McDowell, a first-class musher whose narrow face, high forehead and dashing moustache gave him a passing resemblance to the movie star William Powell. The quartet set out with two dog teams on the morning of December 30, 1931, armed with rifles and sidearms.

They arrived at the cabin on New Year's Eve shortly after daybreak, which occurred about 10:30 a.m. Constable King, a beefy man, approached the cabin in the morning calm. "Are you there, Mr. Johnson?" he called.

The response was a sharp crack as a bullet fired from a .30-30 rifle tore through the closed door and into the officer's chest.

The wounded man staggered for cover. More shots rang out from the cabin, one narrowly missing McDowell. He reached for his Lee Enfield rifle on the sled and returned fire at the hut as his injured partner crawled to safety.

McDowell dumped supplies from the sled to make space for King, the flow of blood from the bullet wound already staunching in the below-freezing temperature. The four officers retreated. The trip to the isolated cabin had taken nearly twenty-eight hours. It seemed unlikely their wounded comrade would survive if the return took that long.

It was a bitterly cold day with howling winds. A desperate flight was made across choppy tundra and into groves of stunted spruce through which trails had to be broken. The men hoisted the sled on several portages before gingerly returning it to the frozen ground. They mushed all through the darkness of New Year's Eve, celebration forgotten in the mad dash to save their comrade.

McDowell completed the 130-kilometre trek to Aklavik in just twenty hours, arriving at the hospital at about 7:00 a.m. on New

Year's Day 1932. His reward was a shot of brandy at the RCMP detachment, while his friend underwent surgery.

Inspector Alexander Eames then led a posse of seven men, including McDowell, which was joined along the way by Charlie Rat, a Native guide. They were accompanied by forty-two dogs, and among the supplies was nine kilograms of dynamite.

They arrived at the hermit's cabin to find it occupied and fortified. Once again, Johnson refused to answer calls to surrender. Instead, he fired through small holes in the walls as the posse riddled the cabin with bullets. After several hours of gunplay, Inspector Eames ordered some of the dynamite to be thawed, a difficult job under the circumstances.

Sticks were thrown against the cabin. Several failed to ignite, others did little damage. At last, it was decided to toss a large bomb onto the roof. The cabin collapsed in the explosion, but when the policemen approached behind a spotlight, Johnson shot it out.

The fifteen-hour siege was a failure. The posse returned to Aklavik. Meanwhile, the first report of the injured Mountie had been sent to newspapers. The latest developments caused a sensation.

A second posse was formed, including two members of the Royal Canadian Signals, marking the first time that two-way radio had been used in police work in Canada. On January 30, an advance party of four stumbled across Johnson, who shot and killed Const. Edgar (Newt) Millen. The trapper fled across the Richardson Mountains into Yukon.

The RCMP needed help covering so large and inhospitable an expanse of land, so an airplane was called in to help with the search (the first order of its kind for such an operation) and to airlift supplies. Wilfrid (Wop) May flew north in a single-winged Bellanca to join the hunt. May, a bush pilot and First World War fighter ace, was familiar with danger and gunplay: the Red Baron (Manfred von Richthofen) had been chasing him when the legendary German was shot down and killed.

May soon spotted the Mad Trapper's trail on the frozen surface of the Eagle River. On February 17, the banner-headline pursuit of the Mad Trapper finally came to an end when Johnson rounded a bend and came face to face with half the posse. In a shootout witnessed by May circling above, the trapper wounded Staff Sgt. Earl Hersey. Johnson was grievously hurt when a bullet struck ammunition in his pocket, blowing a hole in his hip. The fatal shot was a bullet in the spine. A forty-eight-day, three hundred-kilometre manhunt in frigid Arctic weather was finished.

Police found $2,410 in cash, as well as gold fillings, on the trapper's corpse. He had no documents on his person or in his cabin, and his real identity has remained a mystery for eighty years. Although reporters dubbed Johnson "the Mad Trapper," there was no evidence he was insane. In fact, he was highly skilled at Arctic survival and, in his desperate flight, had achieved an astounding midwinter crossing of the Richardson Mountains.

Books about the case have proved popular. *The Death of Albert Johnson*, by F.W. Anderson and three other authors, has sold steadily in several editions since first being published in 1968. Less successful was the 1981 movie *Death Hunt*, which starred Charles Bronson and Lee Marvin.

George Robert McDowell was one of nine children born to parents who worked a modest market garden in St. Vital, Manitoba. The parents fled after the disastrous Red River flood of 1950, settling on an orchard in the small Okanagan town of Oliver. After enlisting in the RCMP as a teenager in 1927, McDowell served in the Northwest Territories before he was selected for a posting at Canada House in London. He also had later postings in Atlantic Canada. He retired with the rank of corporal in 1955, joining his parents on their British Columbia orchard, by which time he had lost all four fingers on his right hand—not from frostbite in the Far North, but from an accident with a paper shredder in a Halifax office.

March 15, 2003

BUSINESS

Jim Spilsbury is credited for bringing news of the world to many of the hamlets and fjords of Canada's Pacific Northwest, and for giving the people living there a way of getting out via his "accidental airlines" company. PHOTO COURTESY OF THE ESTATE OF JIM SPILSBURY

JIM SPILSBURY

SALESMAN, AVIATOR
(OCTOBER 8, 1905—APRIL 20, 2003)

Jim Spilsbury was an itinerant radio salesman and founder of what became known as "the accidental airline." His businesses brought the wider world to the isolated canneries, logging camps, steamer camps and Native villages along the rugged British Columbia coast.

Spilsbury took it as his calling to make life easier for his fellow coast dwellers. He later realized to his dismay that he had contributed to ending a way of life, as many of his customers forsook the hardships of isolation for the city.

The coastal hamlets he visited by boat and, later, plane became a roll call of ghost towns and all-but-forgotten ports of call: Surge Narrows, Blind Channel, Grassy Bay, Squirrel Cove, Whaletown.

"Nowadays the world I knew has all but vanished," he wrote. "As I cruise the bays and inlets I have known so well, the coast for me becomes a haunted place, haunted by all the people and places that gave it life."

Two memoirs he wrote with Howard White became regional bestsellers. *Spilsbury's Coast* won a BC Book Prize, while *The Accidental Airline* was also well received by critics and readers. The cover of both books featured pastels of Pacific coastal scenes by Spilsbury, an accomplished artist.

That he was a proficient storyteller and superb radio technician made him a legendary character long before his books were published. Spilsbury's arrival by boat was a welcome respite from day-to-day labours for many living and working the fjords along the Inside Passage between Vancouver Island and the mainland.

Ashton James Spilsbury was born in the same upstairs bedroom as had been his father at Longlands, the family's ancestral home at Findern, Derbyshire. His parents had returned to the mother country from British Columbia at the urging of the Spilsbury clan, who did not wish to have a scion born in the colonies.

His father, Ashton Wilmot Spilsbury, was a Cambridge-educated gentleman whose modest business schemes were fraught with disaster; his mother, the former Alice Maud Blizard, was a pants-wearing suffragist with little use for convention. Soon after their son's birth, they returned to their 144-hectare British Columbia homestead at Whonnock on the Fraser River.

After a failed business venture cost the family its land, they resettled on Savary Island, a narrow sandbar in Georgia Strait. The Spilsburys made their home in a canvas tent erected on an unused road right-of-way; they were squatters.

Spilsbury got his first formal schooling on the island in September 1914, a month before his ninth birthday. He would attend classes for only four years. By 1919, he began an apprenticeship with a steamship company, an unfortunate choice, as he was seasick for much of the next six months, before quitting.

He worked on Savary as a swamper and knotter on a log float before earning his donkey engineer's steam ticket. When he joined his father in business as Spilsbury and Son, their letterhead included a lengthy list of talents from well-digging to real-estate sales. They also ran a taxi service.

Spilsbury had been fascinated with radio as a teenager, building his first crystal set at age seventeen. The early days of radio involved communication by Morse code. The advent of voice transmission, including a memorable night in 1922 when he tuned in an orchestra performing live from the Fairmont Hotel in San Francisco, turned his interest into an obsession.

In 1926, Spilsbury set out as a radio technician on the *Mary*, a leaky codfish boat rented for a dollar a day. He scrambled to make a living by trolling coastal hamlets and work camps, much of what little profit he made coming from sweet-talking lonely housewives into purchasing an inexpensively produced lemon-oil polish at seventy-five cents a bottle.

The business grew over the years, as Spilsbury sold brand-name radios, as well as those of his own construction, to people for whom the instrument was their only daily contact with the rest of the world. In 1936, he bought a new boat, which he christened the *Five B.R.*, after his ham-radio call of VE5BR.

As a ham operator, he once stayed awake forty consecutive hours as part of a relay of operators from Vancouver through Parksville on Vancouver Island to Spilsbury on Savary Island to Vernon in the Okanagan in the Interior of British Columbia, where a passenger train had derailed in an ice storm. Spilsbury handled 340 messages in three days on his home-built radio.

The *Five B.R.* was called "the radio boat" and was a fixture along the coast, where Spilsbury heralded his arrival by sounding an ear-splitting police siren.

A wartime restriction on gas for boats led him to purchase a Waco Standard biplane for $2,500. Service calls that had taken days now lasted only minutes. "I knew I would never be able to look at that coastal world in quite the same way," he wrote in *Spilsbury's Coast*. "It had become less mysterious, less forbidding, less grand."

Spilsbury soon discovered that those in isolated locales wanted not just radios and repairs, but access to his airplane. He got a charter licence, and bought a pair of twin-engine Stranraer flying boats converted into passenger craft after getting a contract to serve logging companies on the Queen Charlotte Islands.

The ungainly Strannies gave birth to Queen Charlotte Airlines Limited, which took as its slogan, "In the wake of the war canoes." The airline bought so many second-hand aircraft that a separate company was formed to buy and sell equipment. Some said the initials QCA actually stood for Queer Collection of Aircraft. By June 1949, only two other companies—Trans-Canada Airlines and Canadian Pacific—were flying more revenue miles than Spilsbury's accidental airline, which had grown to three hundred employees during the postwar boom.

The company replaced the ugly-duckling Strannies with sleek DC-3s, but the airline struggled as Russ Baker of Central BC Airlines, later Pacific Western, lured passengers away. The upstart bought Queen Charlotte Airlines for $1.4-million in July 1955, by which time Spilsbury was a minority shareholder in the airline he had founded. He was out of the airline business just as suddenly as he had got into it.

He continued manufacturing communications equipment at a converted warehouse in Vancouver. Spilsbury and Tindall Ltd. was a name known around the globe; their famous SBX-11 portable radio telephone was used at the North Pole as well as at the summit of Mount Everest.

Spilsbury was named to the Order of British Columbia in 1993. He was also inducted into the BC Aviation Hall of Fame. An award bearing his name is presented annually by the Coast Guard Auxiliary and the Western Canada Telecommunications Council (which he founded) to the person who contributes the most to marine safety through the use of radio.

Some of Spilsbury's business ventures displayed his father's touch. He lost an estimated $65,000 trying to sell the two-seat Isetta, a microcar nicknamed "the rolling egg."

June 3, 2003

VAL WARREN

NEWSPAPER VISIONARY

(JANUARY 15, 1923—JUNE 25, 2002)

Val Warren saw the future of newspapers buried in a note at the end of a short story in a trade magazine: A newfangled offset press was under development for daily newspapers. Warren grabbed the Canadian rights to the new press and announced he was going to start a third daily newspaper in Vancouver.

He thought he was going to make a fortune. Instead, he lost one.

The story of Warren's ill-fated *Vancouver Times* follows the trajectory of a fireworks shell: A loud, colourful debut, followed by lots of sparks and, finally, ashes. The *Times*, launched on September 5, 1964, would not last a year.

Born in Winnipeg in 1923, William Val Warren enlisted in the Royal Canadian Air Force as an aerial photographer during the Second World War. After his discharge, he joined the newsreel division of the National Film Board. He was on his way to a job in Hollywood when he stopped in Vancouver to visit relatives. He never made it to California.

Warren, who was also known as Bill, handled advertising for small local companies. One of his promotional schemes was a free weekly shopper called the *Metro Times* whose clients grumbled about the high cost of advertising in the two local dailies, the morning *Province* and afternoon *Sun*.

The *Province*, owned by Southam, and the *Sun*, owned in 1964 by Max Bell's FP Publications, had combined to form Pacific Press Ltd. in a new plant on Granville Street. While their editorial staffs remained in competition, the ostensible rivals shared a press and were in cahoots in ways outsiders could only imagine.

Warren had estimated that starting a third daily would cost as much as $15 million. After he got the rights to the French-built offset press distributed by R. Hoe and Co., he figured launching a new daily would cost no more than $5 million.

Offset was a new process in which stenographers hardly more skilled than typists set type photographically on thin sheets of plastic. "Cold type," as it was called, allowed for crisper images and sharper colour than permitted by clunky "hot type." Offset, which was in use by weeklies and small-circulation dailies, was a revolution in printing.

"This was the breakthrough that formed the trenches for the invasion of the newspaper world," Warren said.

Critics warned that offset was too slow for the needs of a big-city daily and too finicky for a publication whose advertisers needed to be on the streets at a guaranteed time. Warren would not hear it. He set up a booth at the Pacific National Exhibition and more than thirty thousand fairgoers signed up to become charter subscribers. The promise of a newspaper with full-colour photographs and magazine-like clarity won over a city where, then as now, the newspapers had no shortage of critics.

"It's fallen into place like a jigsaw puzzle," Warren told *Maclean's* magazine in 1963. "A year ago I was still guessing, but now I know we can't miss."

One of the more interesting innovations was that the broadsheet *Times* would be wrapped around a daily tabloid section featuring sports or entertainment.

Warren's optimism verged on cockiness. "I can smell what people want," he said.

A solid newsroom staff was recruited, with Bill Forst as editorial director, Peter Inglis as editor, Geoffrey Molyneux as managing editor and Mike Tytherleigh as magazine editor. All were former *Province* men, as was Aubrey Roberts, the assistant publisher. Among the paper's stars was a young, bright sportswriter from Victoria named Jim Taylor. The International Typographical Union became the sole representative of all the crafts, compared with a hodge-podge of unions at Pacific Press.

The venerable Major-General Victor Odlum, former owner of the sensationalistic *Daily Star*, which folded in 1932, was coaxed from retirement to become chairman of the board of the Times Publishing Company Ltd.

The newspaper moved into a converted Volkswagen dealership on the east side of Vancouver, far from downtown.

On September 5, 1964, the inaugural *Vancouver Times* appeared amid much hoopla with seventy thousand subscribers and eight hundred carriers whose accounts were handled by—of all things!—a computer.

Warren brashly predicted he would launch five more dailies in Canada over the next seven years.

"They used to say we wouldn't get off the ground," he told *Saturday Night* magazine. "Now they're trying to say we won't last. Well, we've got off the ground and there is no chance of us going broke for the next ten years. Failure is impossible."

Even at his greatest moment of triumph, however, Warren's notices were unkind. Magazine profiles described him as "a hard-driving and humourless ad man," "a much-scorned, cigar-smoking, stocky man," "mildly prosperous and publicly unknown," who was "taunted and mocked as an inexperienced babe in the newsprint."

The success of the first sixty-six-page issue was tainted. The presses proved troublesome and printing was slow. The demand was such that copies were unavailable at newsstands. Some were stolen from doorsteps. More troubling was a lack of advertising.

The newspaper was soon in financial difficulty, as most of the $3 million raised by selling shares had been exhausted in starting up. As well, the board became angry at sweetheart deals Warren had prepared for himself, according to Marc Edge's account in *Pacific Press*, an unauthorized history published in 2001. Warren paid himself a $51,178 salary as publisher, took $75,000 as goodwill for closing his free shopper, and claimed $37,000 in expenses for creating a pilot edition of the *Times*.

The *Times* became desperate, running front-page editorials slamming reluctant advertisers and critical readers. Even the recruitment of popular radio hotline host Pat Burns, the original Mouth That Roared, whose signature greeting was "Go ahead, doll," could not save the fledgling daily. It announced plans to go weekly, then, after Warren was pushed out, published its final issue on August 6, 1965, under the headline "We're taking a pause."

The *Times* had failed, yet Warren's vision proved prophetic. His newspaper, short-lived though it was, was a blueprint of the daily of the future: printed by offset, in full colour, with tabloid supplements, based in offices away from the downtown core.

Warren spent his later working life on product development and venture-capital funding projects.

Warren was not above telling stories in which he served as the butt. The ad man once convinced a dog-food manufacturer to pitch his product as being "fit for human consumption." As recounted in *Saturday Night*, the client and Warren admired a sample can. "Okay, Val," the client finally said, "eat it."

August 20, 2002

Cecil H. Green

CO-FOUNDER, TEXAS INSTRUMENTS

(AUGUST 6, 1900—APRIL 11, 2003)

Cecil Green struggled through early years of near poverty, then spent the last half of his long life giving away the fortune he made from transistor radios and integrated circuits. Green, who died of pneumonia in La Jolla, California, aged 102, was the last living member of the quartet who founded Texas Instruments.

Over the years, Green donated an estimated $200-million US. The largesse fulfilled his wife's wish to one day be a philanthropist, a dream entertained even as the couple ate their meals over a crate in a shack in the Texas backcountry where Green earned $15 a month.

The Greens funded hospitals, colleges, universities, scholarships, professorships, and a vast array of programs in Britain, Canada, Australia and the United States. The affable businessman, known for his long speeches and inexhaustible generosity, began his unlikely rags-to-riches odyssey as a schoolboy in Vancouver.

Cecil Howard Green was born in Whitefield, near Manchester, England, during the reign of Queen Victoria. He was the son of an electrician, Charles Green. The family sailed for Canada when Cecil was aged two, living briefly in Halifax, Montreal and Toronto, before moving to California. Charles Green was still unable to find steady work, so he went north to Vancouver, leaving his wife and

Cecil H. Green may have lived through poor years early in his life, but the eventual co-founder of Texas Instruments earned such a fortune over his life that he donated roughly $200-million US before his death. He sat as president of Geophysical Services Incorporated (GSI) between 1951–55, which is the period when this photo was taken. PHOTO COURTESY OF TEXAS INSTRUMENTS son behind in San Francisco. On the morning of April 18, 1906, they experienced a day never to be forgotten.

"I woke up in the morning with plaster falling on my face," Green recalled in a 1983 interview. "My mother called for help so we could get the door open—the frame, the whole house was twisted. We finally made it out with whatever personal belongings we could carry and weren't allowed back in. We watched the whole city burn."

The terrible earthquake left much of their adopted city in ruins. Nearly eight decades later, Green vividly recalled a soldier breaking a store window to snatch a pair of shoes so the barefooted boy could walk safely along glass-strewn streets.

His mother, Maggie, secured a pair of one-way northbound tickets and left the city. In later years, Cecil Green would jokingly tell the story as an explanation for his lifelong interest in seismology. His friends heard in the tale a harbinger of many events.

He attended Edith Cavell elementary and King Edward High in Vancouver. "The system was tops," he once said. "Tough, rigorous, always stimulating." He entered the University of British Columbia as an arts student, transferring to sciences as a sophomore. After three years, a chemistry professor convinced Green to attend the Massachusetts Institute of Technology (MIT). He earned a bachelor of science degree in electrical engineering at MIT in 1923 and a master's degree the following year. He designed steam turbine generators as a research engineer for General Electric in Schenectady, New York, where he met Ida Mabelle Flansburgh, a statistician whom he married on February 6, 1926. He always called her Miss Ida. In return, she addressed him as, simply, Green.

He made electronic rectifiers for Raytheon Manufacturing Co. in Cambridge, Massachusetts, before returning to Vancouver, a city he frequently proclaimed "the most beautiful place on earth." His ardour was not repaid at first, as his attempts to launch a neon-sign company failed. He then briefly sold a newfangled car accessory—turn signals—in Seattle.

At last, he found work as an assistant to the hard-charging

Charles Litton at the electronics firm Federal Telegraph Co. in Palo Alto, California. The men laboured daily into the early-morning hours, a gruelling pace that Ida Green was unwilling to allow her husband to maintain. Litton went on to found electronics giant Litton Industries; Green was hired as field-crew chief by Geophysical Service Inc., a Dallas company helping clients find oil deposits through the untried field of reflection seismology.

The next years were spent as a doodlebug, wandering the dusty backroads of Texas, Louisiana and Oklahoma, temporarily living in such out-of-the-way hamlets as Stillwater, Oklahoma. Despite his low wage and their modest circumstances, the childless couple dreamed of someday giving away yet-to-be-earned riches.

When the company was offered for sale, Green joined associates Eugene McDermott, J. Erik Jonsson and H. Bates Peacock in contributing $300,000 each for the purchase. Green had to mortgage all his property to raise his share. The sale was completed on December 6, 1941. News of the Japanese attack on Pearl Harbor came the next morning. Fearing their employees would be inducted into the army, the new owners decided to abandon oil exploration in favour of becoming a protected war industry. Among their most useful electronic products was a submarine detection device.

In 1950, Green became president of the company, which soon after changed its name to Texas Instruments. The company entered the semiconductor business in 1952, produced the first mass-market pocket radio in 1954, and heralded a new age of electronics by developing the integrated circuit in 1958.

The company's growth was phenomenal. Texas Instruments went public on October 1, 1953, selling shares at $5.25. By May 1960, shares were trading at $210 each.

Green was chairman of the board from 1956–59, and honorary chairman afterwards.

The scope of the couple's charity was as staggering as their personal frugality. Over the years, they donated more than $31.7-million US to MIT alone.

The names Cecil H. and Ida M. Green are well known

throughout English-speaking academe, as they endowed professorships at leading institutions, financed innovative programs and created entire colleges. Such donations were not entirely selfless. For instance, an orientation program in exploratory geophysics involving MIT, the Colorado School of Mines and the University of Toronto served as a talent pool from which recruits for his firm were scouted.

Green was awarded more than a dozen honorary degrees, and he was presented countless medals, awards, tributes and citations, including having been named a freeman of the city of Vancouver in 1987. On May 22, 1991, Queen Elizabeth bestowed on Green an honorary knighthood.

William C. Gibson, a professor emeritus at UBC, helped re-acquaint Green with his alma mater. The philanthropist had retained a fond feeling for the city that had been his home for sixteen years, although he had yet to visit the university's Point Grey campus. On a tour, Green spotted a mansion across the street from the university and decided to buy it. The house, designed by renowned architect Samuel Maclure and built in 1912, was originally named Kanakla ("house on the cliff"). It is now known as Cecil Green Park House.

In 1972, the couple began financing the Cecil and Ida Green Visiting Professorship program at UBC. Gibson also convinced his well-heeled friend to finance a Green College at Oxford, as well as one at UBC, which opened in 1993 as a graduate student centre. "He used to call me his most expensive friend," Gibson told me.

Green died at a hospital that carries his name in La Jolla, California. He was predeceased by his wife, who died at the same hospital in 1986.

May 29, 2003

Trev Deeley was a motorcycle man, as can be seen in this 1946 photo of him sitting on a hillclimber. He started out as a successful racer and grew to become an innovative businessman, earning the nickname, "Motorcycle Millionaire." PHOTO COURTESY OF THE DEELEY MOTORCYCLE EXHIBITION

TREV DEELEY

MOTORCYCLE DEALER
(MARCH 15, 1920—MARCH 28, 2002)

Mourners marking the death of Trev Deeley dressed in black—black leather. A gathering in Deeley's honour attracted both outlaw bikers and motorcycle cops, sworn enemies who put aside their animosity for the sake of a man whose name was synonymous with motorcycles on the West Coast.

He was called "Daredevil Deeley" as a young man, and he died, aged eighty-two, known as the Motorcycle Millionaire.

A champion racer, Deeley became a spectacularly successful businessman by midlife. His passion was expressed in horsepower, but his genius was in anticipating the response of potential motorcycle buyers to new models.

In the late 1950s, Deeley was the first to import sporty Japanese motorcycles to Canada. Later, he sold Harley-Davidsons to salve the midlife crises of aging baby boomers.

He rode his own Harley whenever he could, perhaps finding on the open road respite from a cruel father and a life scarred by tragic loss. Deeley buried an infant son and, nine years later, a wife who died from the complications of childbirth. His tormenting father lived to be eighty-four.

Frederick Trevor Deeley was born in Vancouver to a teenaged

couple who had been married less than three months. His father, Frederick Granville Deeley, known as Fred Jr., had tried to run away when Islay Jeanne Segwick, daughter of a streetcar motorman, announced her pregnancy, but his family marched him to the altar.

Family patriarch Alfred Deeley had been born in Bromsgrove, south of Birmingham, England, moving his brood to Canada in 1914. "Fred Deeley, the Cycle Man" also sold British motorbikes until the Great War caused a shortage. Then he began to import Harley-Davidson machines from the United States.

Trev Deeley was first photographed atop a motorcycle at age two. He would later quip that he had been born in a sidecar. According to biographer Frank Hilliard, Deeley's first actual ride came when he was seven, although he didn't know how to stop the machine. Bystanders grabbed the bike to disengage the clutch.

He quit school in Grade 10 to work for the family firm, where one of his early jobs was repossessing motorcycles during the Depression.

Soon after, he began to salvage old machines, which the company had been selling for scrap at fifty cents a pound. Intimidated by his father, Deeley kept the collection a secret for decades.

He joined the army reserve with fellow motorcycle-club members after being asked to aid police in providing crowd control during the royal visit of 1939. Two years later, he was called up to serve with the Royal Canadian Ordnance Corps in Calgary. Deeley got a medical discharge for asthma in 1943, finding work in Vancouver delivering telegrams by motorcycle.

After he and Vera Wasilieff were married, Deeley visited his wife's family aboard a powerful, new machine, and his father-in-law, who had been a motorcycle dispatch rider in the First World War, took the bike for a spin. He crashed and died.

Deeley nearly killed himself at a hill-climbing competition, yet over the years managed to avoid serious injury despite showing a pugnacious streak both on the track and off.

With wavy black hair worn short and a cocky grin on his face, Deeley (who looked like *Hogan's Heroes* star Robert Crane) made racer No. 22 a respected but not always beloved competitor. "The willingness to put in an elbow, cut off an opponent or ride another competitor into the rail became one of Trevor's characteristics," Hilliard wrote in his 1994 biography, *Deeley: Motorcycle Millionaire.*

He won regional championships in Western Canada and the US Pacific Northwest. Among his many triumphs was the notorious Death Head Derby in Lacey, Washington, where the trophy was a human skull found when the local track was built. He also raced at the famous sand-and-highway course at Daytona Beach, Florida, throwing a rooster-tail cloud of dirt over spectators with his aggressive cornering, and was a factory rider for Harley-Davidson.

After a difficult pregnancy, Vera Deeley gave birth to the couple's first child, a son, on September 1, 1948. Timothy Trevor suffered severe anemia and was in hospital when his father won the Alcan Cup at the Western Canada championship in Edmonton on Labour Day weekend. He died September 8, shortly after his father came home.

In 1957, after giving birth prematurely to a baby girl, Vera Deeley died of heart failure. Dawne Elizabeth was raised by her father's parents.

Earlier that year, Deeley had been intrigued by a magazine photograph of a US serviceman riding a Japanese-built motorcycle. He wrote several letters to the company, which at last delivered a blue 250cc Honda Dream. That machine was to alter a market that had been dominated by British, American and, to a lesser degree, Italian bikes.

Deeley is said to have been first in the English-speaking world to import the Japanese machines. He did so initially over the objection of his father and the incredulous reaction of his network of dealers.

The Hondas proved hugely popular. (The easy ignition made it a favoured purchase for women frustrated by kick-starting.) He had correctly anticipated the demand for a stylish, well-engineered machine unsullied by the brutish reputation given riders by such movies as *The Wild One*. He also hired top young riders to race Hondas to victory.

Meanwhile, Deeley's private life became ever more messy. He fell in love with a married woman whom he eventually wed after her divorce was finalized. The union lasted only another eighteen months.

Later, he took up with another married woman, and in the middle of one night, found himself in a fist fight with the husband of the woman with whom he was sharing a bed. The fisticuffs persuaded the husband his marriage was over, allowing Deeley to wed the former Joyce Ogilvie, daughter of a Victoria store manager.

Despite his business savvy, Deeley continued to endure his father's domineering manner, while his younger brother, Ray, struck out on his own, and became the national distributor of Suzuki motorcycles.

Trev Deeley and Honda finally parted company—he concluded a dispute with the company by selling the franchise to take over distribution of Yamaha motorcycles and snowmobiles. Once again, he put together a top-notch racing team, winning the world superbike championship in 1976.

After twelve years of handling Yamaha products, he switched again. Long a fan of Harley-Davidsons, he became the American firm's exclusive Canadian distributor, once more correctly anticipating a new market—aging baby boomers with the money, the time and the spirit for one last kick at the open road.

For the first time, he was operating on his own (although calling his company Fred Deeley Imports suggested he was backed by his family's millions), and in 1985 became a member of the Harley-Davidson board of directors. He also helped design and critique new models and, late in life, was recognized for his contributions to the sport. He was inducted into the Canadian Motorsport Hall of Fame in 1996; the Motorcycle Hall of Fame at Pickerington, Ohio, in 1999; and the BC Sports Hall of Fame in 2000.

Joyce Deeley died of cancer in March 2001. A year earlier, the couple had made a million-dollar donation toward a research wing at the new Vancouver Island Cancer Centre. Deeley died at his waterfront home in the Victoria suburb of North Saanich on March 28, 2002.

A month later, about three thousand motorcyclists gathered to celebrate his life, with members of the Hells Angels and police motorcycle drill teams among them. Deeley had sold Harleys to both. The farewell was held beside the Deeley corporate offices in suburban Richmond, which also house the Trev Deeley Motorcycle Museum. The once-secret collection is now a shrine to a man who said of motorcycling: "It's all that I've ever known."

June 1, 2002

JAMES WALLACE

NEON SIGNMAKER

(DECEMBER 13, 1920—SEPTEMBER 25, 2002)

The neon signs owned by James Wallace once lit the Vancouver sky. Seen by some as garish, they became museum pieces and icons of local pop culture.

A mere listing of businesses illuminated by a Wallace Neon sign evokes nostalgia in residents of a certain age—the Ovaltine Cafe, the Ho Ho Chop Suey restaurant, the Smilin' Buddha cabaret.

Wallace's company also produced memorable works for the Dragon Inn restaurant, the Save On Meats butcher shop, the Admiral Hotel and the Home Oil gas barge moored off Stanley Park.

The city's neon heritage has been celebrated in recent years, including a well-received show called City Lights, which opened at the Vancouver Museum in 1999.

The star of that show was the famed cabaret sign, which includes a grinning Buddha in a robe. The Buddha's ample belly has parallel curves that blink in sequence, giving the appearance of jiggling while laughing. The critic Robin Ward once said the sign had been "drawn with a casual Matisse-like line."

The band 54-40 titled a 1994 album after the Smilin' Buddha

Cabaret, including the neon sign as the cover art. The actual sign was displayed on stage during live performances.

However, not everyone appreciates the qualities of neon. Over the years, Wallace defended his signs against those who sought to beautify the city by getting rid of what they saw as gaudy advertising. In 1966, Wallace appeared before Vancouver city council to defend a blinking sign at a major intersection. "A sign without animation and changing colour is like TV without sound, like radio without music, like newspapers without pictures," he told council. He would ultimately lose the battle.

James Bertram Wallace, who was born in Vancouver, returned from war service in North Africa to join his father's firm at the end of the Second World War. Wallace began as a sign painter and later would become president and owner of the firm.

The first neon sign was sold in Vancouver in 1928 by Neon Products Ltd. Wallace Neon arose as its major competitor, although a dozen companies shared a booming market.

By the late 1940s, Wallace's company employed six artists whose visions were brought to life by skilled fabricators, blowers, benders, electricians and painters, the artist Keith McKellar wrote in *Neon Eulogy*, an illustrated, book-length homage published in 2001. The shop boasted a twenty-two by eighty foot T-square that slid on rails.

Wallace Neon signs were notable both for their craftsmanship and the wit of their design. The Ho Ho sign included chopsticks jutting from a steaming bowl of noodles, the restaurant's name appearing in both Roman script and Chinese characters within steam rising several stories. The Save On Meats sign depicts a penny-pinching pig dancing a jig.

The signs were owned by Wallace Neon and leased to businesses, making a new sign affordable to a storeowner in the short term and profitable to the manufacturer in the long term.

Neon was extremely popular in Vancouver. So many signs lit the Granville Street shopping areas that it was described as the "Great White Way of the West Coast." In 1958, the city's often gloomy skies were lit by about eighteen thousand neon signs.

The signs also attracted critics, who complained they detracted from the city's natural setting. In 1974, city council banned all new neon except small, unblinking window displays. Two years later, Wallace Neon was sold to Sicon, a company best known by its Sign-O-Lite trade name.

Wallace owned a farm along the Nicomekl River in the Vancouver suburb of Surrey, where he was twice elected as an alderman. As a philanthropist, he made donations to the local hospital as well as to the University of British Columbia and the Lester B. Pearson College of the Pacific.

He was also a breeder and owner of thoroughbred race horses, many of which found the winner's circle at Exhibition (now Hastings) Park in Vancouver. He was a member of the Rolls Royce Owners' Club and the Royal Vancouver Yacht Club. He retired as a pilot after surviving a crash-landing.

At age seventy-six, he donated $25,000 for a study on the feasibility of re-introducing passenger service along an interurban railroad through Surrey. He believed the return of electric passenger cars would ease traffic congestion as well as boost tourism.

The BC Electric Railway once ran from New Westminster through Surrey to Chilliwack in the Fraser Valley, linking the city to farmland. The route, opened in 1910, had been abandoned in 1950. In recent years, the eighty-kilometre length of track, which now connects burgeoning bedroom communities, was used only twice daily by a freight train.

Wallace's one-man campaign eventually inspired Surrey City Council to approve a $5-million, ten-year interurban rail plan. Surrey spent $200,000 in 2001 to restore a heritage rail car, build a car barn in the Cloverdale neighbourhood and upgrade twenty-one kilometres of track. As a boy, Wallace had travelled by electric rail car to Vancouver. He remembered the heavy rail cars gently rocking back and forth—"like a lullaby," he said.

December 13, 2002

JEAN CROWLEY

DAIRY OWNER
(OCTOBER 13, 1913—SEPTEMBER 16, 2004)

A cold, glass bottle of milk—an object simple in its science and peerless in its pleasure—saved Jean Crowley's dairy business from souring like so many others.

Crowley spent more than six decades fighting to preserve what is now the oldest family-run dairy in British Columbia. She succeeded, in part, with a stubborn insistence on bottling fresh milk in glass.

Avalon Dairy survived its leanest years thanks to customers interested in natural foods and hygienic packaging. A niche market grew in recent years as nostalgia helped fuel the desire for wholesome foods. By being old-fashioned, Avalon became a trendsetter. "Sticking to glass bottles, of course, was a perverse decision," Crowley once told me. "But we had no choice." She nursed the business through years of great change in the industry, as bottles gave way to cartons, gallons gave way to litres, and horse-drawn wagons gave way to trucks measured in horsepower.

At the same time, dozens of family dairies were swallowed by a handful of large companies. In 1948, Vancouver had eighty-four independents. By 1966, it had just one.

The dairy, at 5805 Wales Street in Vancouver's Collingwood

Jean Crowley's efforts not only kept Avalon Dairy afloat during lean years, but also kept it as the last standing independent dairy in Vancouver—ensuring that a dairy farm that had started before she was born would continue on even after she died. PHOTO BY DAN SCOTT, PROVIDED BY THE *VANCOUVER SUN*

neighbourhood, is a reminder of the city's agricultural roots. Originally set amid orchards, hobby farms and forest, the dairy is now surrounded by acres of bungalows and boxy houses known as Vancouver Specials. Crowley raised her children on the dairy's grounds in a whitewashed farmhouse set on an expanse of lawn.

Jean Marguerite Fraser grew up in the eastside Vancouver neighbourhood of Cedar Cottage. She attended John Oliver High School before graduating with a bachelor of science degree from the University of British Columbia in 1932. Her area of expertise was bacteriology.

She worked at Vancouver General Hospital after graduation. In August 1938, she married Everett (Ev) Crowley at Cedar Cottage United Church before embarking on a three-week honeymoon in the Rocky Mountains. The couple would make several notable automobile journeys in their life, including a "See B.C. First Caravan" sponsored by the Junior Board of Trade to promote tourism in the province in 1946.

Ev Crowley was the seventh of thirteen children born to Maud and Jeremiah Crowley, a metal worker from Western Bay on Newfoundland's Avalon Peninsula. Jeremiah Crowley, a pipe-smoking, bowler-wearing eccentric with a reputation as a harsh taskmaster, moved the family to the West Coast in 1906 to pursue life as a farmer. He bought a hectare of land—and six cows—for $4,000. The original farm, named the Avalon Dairy Ranch, was built at the site of what is now Norquay Park, moving to the current address three years later.

An outbreak of bovine tuberculosis in 1931 forced the family to slaughter their dairy herd. Ever after, raw milk for bottling has been trucked in from farms in the Fraser Valley. After barely surviving the Depression, the dairy thrived during the Second World War, thanks to subsidies, price controls and the increased demand for milk.

Meanwhile, a booming city was encroaching on the dairy. Residential neighbours complained about the sour smell of unwanted skim milk poured down city drains. Their crying over spilt milk was not merely a matter of aesthetics; the disposal was attracting rats. A series of squabbles with the city led Ev Crowley to become politically active. In 1947, he came to be known as Poll Tax Ev during a well-publicized campaign against a $5 levy. His refusal to pay won him a three-day jail sentence. He served only two, being released a day early for good behaviour. He also ran unsuccessfully in several provincial elections. In 1957, he finished fourth as a federal Liberal in the riding of Vancouver Kingsway.

Meanwhile, Jean Crowley launched her own political career with greater success. She topped the polls as a Non-Partisan Association candidate for school board in 1955, earning more votes in the city-wide election than any other candidate for any civic office ever had. She became chair of the school board in 1959, a launching pad for a future bid to win a seat in the provincial legislature. In 1966, Jean Crowley challenged Social Credit incumbents Grace McCarthy and Leslie Peterson in the two-member riding of Vancouver–Little Mountain. Crowley, running for the provincial Liberal party, got just 4,270 votes of more than 50,000 cast, finishing last of six candidates. After that disappointment, she became an active political organizer, becoming president of the federal Liberal association in her home riding.

As well, Crowley helped destitute women as a founding member of the East Enders Society. She also was a lifetime member of the Provincial Council of Women, serving as the group's president from 1971 to 1974.

Over those years, major changes took place at the dairy. The last delivery horse was retired in 1953. Daily home deliveries were replaced with a skip-a-day routine in 1965 before being cancelled in 1973. What remained the same was a reliance on glass bottles, an industrial package long since abandoned by rivals. The Crowleys even made a cross-country trek in search of glass bottles to replenish a dwindling stock.

By 1975, the dairy was bottling just 364 litres of milk per day, processed one day and delivered the next by youngest son Lee Crowley. The business stayed afloat only by meeting the demand of health-food advocates. The dairy won new customers in 1988 following reports that traces of toxins had been found in cardboard cartons.

Today, the dairy serves another specialty market by bottling certified organic milk produced by cows that roam freely on a farm in Aldergrove.

December 14, 2004

Labour

The day known as "Bloody Sunday" earned its name for the blood Robert Brodie lost during the beating he received from police after organizing a sit-down strike in the post office. He has his hands on his head after being evicted from that sit-down strike in 1938. PROVINCE NEWSPAPER PHOTO PROVIDED BY VANCOUVER PUBLIC LIBRARY, 41609

ROBERT (STEVE) BRODIE

LABOURER, SEAMAN, ORGANIZER
(JUNE 8, 1910—DECEMBER 6, 2007)

A man can pack a lot of living into eighty-seven years, and Steve Brodie didn't waste any of them. Yet for all that he did and all that he saw in his time, he was remembered for what happened one dawn seven decades ago, when four Mounties with billy clubs and a Vancouver city detective armed with a rubber hose beat the living bejeezus out of him. It was June 19, 1938—Bloody Sunday—and much of the blood was his.

A month earlier, he had led a contingent of unemployed men into the Vancouver Post Office on a sitdown strike. The way he conducted himself in those days made him the most admired—and feared—man in the city.

As a boy in Scotland, Robert Brodie lost both parents to the influenza epidemic of 1919. Five years later, the Salvation Army shipped him and other orphans to Canada, where he found work at fourteen as a farm labourer.

Brodie was a Bible-quoting believer like his blacksmith father, a lay preacher, but at one farm in the Sand Hills of Saskatchewan he came upon a former journalist with a library of radical books. "He told me, 'You are a member of the working class and you have no option but to help them rise,'" Brodie recalled. "I used to read the

Bible to the Indian girl who lived with him, but I was beginning to doubt."

In the early 1930s, his livelihood evaporated along with the moisture of the Prairie soil. He took to the rails like so many other hungry men. One bitter winter's night, he was hauled aboard a slow-moving freight. An older man dragged him across the dark boxcar and flicked his lighter. At Brodie's feet, as recounted in Pierre Berton's *The Great Depression*, were three teenaged boys, frozen to death.

It was in the relief camps that he was nicknamed "Steve," after the Irishman who was said to have jumped from the Brooklyn Bridge on a bet. In 1935, Steve Brodie hopped a freight in Vancouver with hundreds of others in an audacious protest. The On-to-Ottawa Trek ended when police attacked a crowd on Dominion Day in an event remembered as the Regina Riot.

Brodie came to believe that capitalism made the many miserable for the benefit of a few. (Nothing he saw later caused him to change his opinion.) He joined the Communist Party, which, with its top-down discipline, would prove an uneasy and short-lived fit for the firebrand battler.

On May 20, 1938, some two thousand bedraggled men marched in columns through downtown Vancouver. Brodie led one group into the post office, while others took over the Vancouver Art Gallery and the Georgia Hotel. The men settled in at the post office, sleeping on the cold stone floor. They called it the Hotel Federal. Thousands visited with gifts of food. The pocket-sized *Sitdowner Gazette* was sold to raise money. Meanwhile, the mails kept moving.

Early one morning, the clip-clop of horses' hooves was heard. The police ordered the building vacated; the men, led by Brodie, said they would submit to arrest. The police refused, firing a tear-gas canister. "Up until that moment, we had lived for thirty days in that building without five cents worth of damage to property," Brodie later wrote. "Now as the lobby filled with gas, arrangements were made to purify the air by eliminating some three thousand dollars worth of plate glass."

The sitdowners ran a gantlet of police. The five-foot-eight, 138-pound Brodie was the last man out, his orange sweater a bull's-eye for the waiting cops. He was beaten senseless and left in the gutter. Police refused to call an ambulance. A passerby drove him to St. Paul's Hospital. He had head injuries, nearly lost an eye, and was left toothless.

The eye injury prevented him from serving in the regular forces during the Second World War, which he spent in the merchant marine. He later worked in the Esquimalt shipyards, retiring in 1968. Never married, he was a devoted surrogate grandfather and great-grandfather. As an old man, he would meet cronies at a Victoria cafeteria, where they bet on the ponies and Brodie touted his system for winning at craps with his trademark dry cockiness. He long ago had abandoned any faith in political parties, although he remained as angry at injustice as ever.

The post office he occupied so many years ago is now home to upscale boutiques, the doorways once again temporary refuge for the homeless. Unlike in Brodie's day, they are unorganized and without hope.

January 23, 1998

Homer Stevens claimed he grew crankier with age, and if the scowl this fisherman-turned-union-advocate is wearing in this 1997 photo is any indication of his daily disposition, he was probably telling the truth. PHOTO BY RICK LOUGHRAN, PROVIDED BY THE PROVINCE

Homer Stevens

FISHERMAN

(AUGUST 2, 1923—OCTOBER 2, 2002)

Homer Stevens was a fisherman by trade, a Communist by politics and a rabble-rouser by nature.

Stevens, a figure both admired and despised along the British Columbia coast, was the longtime leader of the United Fishermen and Allied Workers' Union (UFAWU). He was an unwavering advocate for his fellow union fishermen, once spending nearly a year in jail for defying an injunction against picketing. Over the years, he battled judges, companies, rival unions, anti-union fishermen, Red baiters, fellow Communists and anticommunists. He was known for a fiery temperament. Late in life, he acknowledged that he had become progressively crankier as he got older.

He was a tenacious champion of the fishermen's cause. For more than twenty years, Stevens and the union fought to make fishermen eligible for workers' compensation, at long last providing some small solace and sustenance for the widows of the sea. His lifelong dream was to organize one big union representing all fishery workers. He was raised in a fishing port and knew the language and ways of the people whose support he sought. Stevens worked the Vancouver waterfront on foot and by streetcar, making his pitch over a fresh catch on the docks or over a cool pitcher of beer at a hotel pub. He also patrolled the coast in the union's own boat, *Chiquita*, capable of eight knots.

His many successes were reflected in the much-improved lot of fishermen in the years before fish stocks collapsed, yet his failures were somehow even more spectacular. A strike called in Prince Rupert in 1967 ended in decertification, Stevens and the union president were jailed, and the union's coffers were lightened by a $25,000 fine, as well as by damages of $100,000 won in a civil suit by owners of fishing boats.

An attempt to organize the East Coast fishermen in the early 1970s ended in a disaster that would later seem inevitable given the poor financing and planning of the campaign. In part, the sheer desperation of some of the fishermen led to a strike "not of our choosing or timing" that was ultimately lost. He also was no stranger to defeat as an electoral candidate, faring poorly in eight campaigns in which he carried the Communist banner.

Homer John Stevens was the son of a fisherman who was the son of a fisherman. His grandfather, Gjan Giannan, was a Greek seaman whose name was anglicized to John Stevens when he applied for a cannery licence. The first Stevens married an aboriginal woman from Esquimalt named Emma, who would later take little Homer with her in a cedar dugout canoe and teach him the traditional way of fishing by spear.

His mother was the Canadian-born daughter of Croatian immigrants. She had lost a son to drowning and her first husband to the 1919 influenza epidemic before she married Stevens's father in 1921. Homer was born two years later.

He grew up next door to a sawmill and across the street from rows of bunkhouses in Port Guichon, a lively fishing community on the south arm of the Fraser River. Conversations were conducted in English, Songhees, Chinook jargon, Croatian, Italian and Greek. By age thirteen, Homer was operating the gillnetter *Tar Box*, powered by a 3.5-hp engine, on his own. He fished salmon, dogfish, starry flounder, sole and ling cod.

Fishermen belonged to a wide variety of unions and

associations, based on their location, ethnicity and equipment, not to mention ancient rivalries and divisions. In 1941, when he was skipper of a four-man trawler, Stevens's uncle encouraged him to attend a United Fishermen's meeting. "It's run by a bunch of Reds," he remembered his uncle saying, "but they're pretty good people."

Stevens tried to enlist in the air force, but a wonky right eye disqualified him for pilot training. The navy had no more room and he hated the thought of the army, so he stayed on his fishing boat.

He was active in the credit-union movement, as well as the fishermen's co-operative movement, and was an organizer for the Co-operative Commonwealth Federation when he was not working on a dragger in winter, or a gillnetter in the summer and fall.

In 1945, a shoreworkers' union and a fishermen's union merged to form the UFAWU, an acronym that would soon become synonymous with Stevens. He was hired as a full-time organizer the following year and would spend the next three decades with the union. In his eponymous 1992 memoir, written with Rolf Knight, Stevens figured he made $1,800 in his first year with the union, while his friends pulled in as much as $6,000 on the boats.

As a boy, he had taken part in a nasty dispute, with racial overtones, involving Japanese-Canadian fishermen. His father told him that he would not tolerate discrimination, a lesson Stevens never forgot. He took the unpopular decision to argue in favour of allowing interned Japanese-Canadian fishermen to return to the industry on the West Coast after the war. During a union meeting on the issue, a member rose to speak: "I'd made up my mind a long time ago that when the first Jap got back into the fishing industry, I was going to take my rifle and shoot him," the man told Stevens. "But I've changed my mind. When the first one of them comes back, I'm coming over [to] shoot you."

By 1953, the union was under attack by fellow trade unionists. The Trades and Labour Congress suspended the union for "Communist leanings." The fishermen would not be re-admitted to the so-called House of Labour for two decades. Shortly after the suspension, the Seafarers' International began raids on the fishermen's union's locals.

That same year, Stevens made his first electoral foray as the Labour-Progressive Party candidate in Burnaby Richmond. He finished fourth in a tight, three-way race, although his 792 votes were more than the margin separating the CCF and Conservative also-rans from the Liberal victor.

He ran for Parliament on five more occasions as a Communist, the last attempt coming in 1988, when he finished last of eight candidates. He also ran twice as a Communist in provincial elections.

Once, union president Steve Stavenes told Stevens that it would benefit the union if he left the Communist party. "If you want a political eunuch go get somebody else as secretary-treasurer," Stevens said, as recounted in his memoir. "You want my balls? Well, you're not going to have them. Either you accept me as I am or turn me out of office."

Stevens did quit the Communist party for several years, but rejoined.

He wound up in jail after receiving an injunction ordering five strikebound boats be unloaded during the Prince Rupert strike. The union's executive decided to poll the membership, who voted against obeying the court order. Stevens was arrested some time later, convicted of contempt and sentenced to one year in jail. He served eleven months.

"It seemed to me that a judge could order almost anything in an injunction and that he could cite almost anything as being in contempt of his ruling," Stevens wrote in his memoir.

He retired from the union in 1977 with eighteen months of severance pay and no pension. He returned to fishing, although he became seasick on his first venture, much to his embarrassment.

In 1982, Stevens sold a lot next to his house to help cover the cost of buying a boat and licence from BC Packers for $73,000. He named his new boat *Emma S.* to honour the grandmother who had first taught him to fish so many years before.

November 14, 2002

VILLAIN

GILBERT PAUL JORDAN

SERIAL KILLER

(DECEMBER 12, 1931—JULY 7, 2006)

Gilbert Paul Jordan was the "Boozing Barber," a headline nickname for a sexual predator whose weapon was alcohol. At least ten women, most of them aboriginal, spent their final moments of life in his company. He was convicted of manslaughter in the death of just one, a travesty some blamed on racial attitudes held by the police and the courts.

Short in stature, stocky enough as a youth to have been called "Chub" or "Chubby," he was himself an alcoholic capable of consuming enormous quantities of vodka and other intoxicants.

Possessed of a fierce temper, he displayed the qualities of a psychopath. A brother called him a "Jekyll and Hyde," while a Crown prosecutor described him as "cold and manipulative." He had no remorse for killing his victims.

"They were all on their last legs," he once told the reporter Jim Beatty. "I didn't give a damn who I was [drinking] with. I mean, we're all dying sooner or later, whether it's in this bar, across the street or wherever."

Three women died of alcohol poisoning at his barbershop, yet the proprietor was never charged in their deaths.

His undoing was the drinking death of Vanessa Lee Buckner,

whose body was found in a room at the Niagara Hotel in downtown Vancouver. She had a reputation as a social drinker and was not known to binge, yet her blood-alcohol level was a stupefying 0.91, more than eleven times a driver's legal limit of 0.08 and twice the amount capable of causing death.

Suspicion fell on her drinking companion that night. He would be charged with first-degree murder, later reduced to manslaughter. Convicted and sentenced to fifteen years imprisonment, the sentence was reduced to nine years on appeal. He served six.

The case of the Boozing Barber was recounted in chilling detail by a team of *Vancouver Sun* reporters in 1988. They uncovered a startling history of crime without punishment and portrayed a serial killer whose appetite for alcohol and forced sex led to many deaths.

The barber avoided being declared a dangerous offender. Despite court-ordered restrictions on his behaviour, he remained a threat to the vulnerable women among whom he prowled. The RCMP in the Victoria suburb of Saanich issued another in a series of warnings as recently as February 2005.

"Jordan has a significant criminal record including manslaughter and indecent assault of a female," the warning stated. "He uses alcohol to lure his victims.

"Jordan's target victim group is adult females."

Partly bald with grey hair and goatee, his blue eyes showing behind stylish eyeglasses, he would have looked like someone's grandfather if not for a leering smile and the reek of alcohol. He was the author of a sordid chapter in the annals of Canadian crime, a serial killer who mostly evaded punishment and remained a threat to his dying day.

He was also a wealthy barber, claiming to have made savvy investments after receiving a healthy family inheritance. He was certainly able to afford first-rate lawyers.

Raised in Vancouver, Paul Elsie, as he was known, dropped out of high school and began drinking about the time his parents' marriage collapsed. He was, by his own admission, an alcoholic by sixteen.

The *Sun's* investigation uncovered a lengthy criminal record, beginning with a car theft in 1950 and including convictions for theft, assault and heroin possession. He was also a notorious drunk driver who was charged numerous times, including twice on the same day in 1969.

His unlawful behaviour also led to two bizarre incidents reported by local newspapers. Two days after Christmas in 1961, he halted traffic on the Lions Gate Bridge by threatening to jump into Burrard Inlet. Soon after, he disrupted a North Vancouver courtroom by offering Nazi salutes, for which he was found in contempt of court.

More ominously, he began to be charged with—but not convicted of—the kinds of sexual crimes that would earn him his deserved notoriety.

A stay of proceedings in May 1961 ended a case in which he was charged with abduction after a five-year-old aboriginal girl was found in his car far from her reserve.

Two years later, he was acquitted of rape, although found guilty of theft, in an incident involving two women invited to drink in his car.

The *Sun* series, titled "Death by Alcohol" and published in 1988, also reported his involvement in the deaths of ten women. His first victim was Ivy Rose (Doreen) Oswald, an English-born switchboard operator whose nude body was found in a Vancouver hotel room in 1965. Her blood-alcohol reading was 0.51. For twenty-two years, her death had been considered accidental.

Days after her death, her drinking companion applied to have his surname legally changed to Jordan.

Criminal charges continued to pile up over the years, most involving alcohol but also including a dismissed charge of committing an indecent act in a public place in Vancouver (1971) and a conviction for indecent exposure in Mackenzie (1973).

By 1974, he was living in Prince George, where he was sentenced to two years less a day for indecent assault. An application by Crown counsel to have him declared a dangerous sexual offender was denied in 1976. The next year, he was charged with several counts, including kidnapping and sexual intercourse with the feeble-minded, in an incident involving a young woman taken from a mental institution. He was convicted of assault and sentenced to twenty-six months.

It was during a stay in prison that he learned to be a barber. He operated the Slocan Barber Shop on Kingsway Avenue on Vancouver's east side.

He lured women to fleabag hotel rooms or to his untidy shop, where he plied them with alcohol before raping them. Three women would die in the shop of alcohol poisoning from July 1982, to June 1985. Each death was investigated by a coroner, but somehow the barber avoided a criminal investigation.

At 6 a.m. on October 12, 1987, the barber left a room at the Niagara Hotel after a night of drinking. More than an hour later, he called the police emergency line to report a death. He did not give his name. Vanessa Buckner, twenty-seven, who sometimes worked as a prostitute, had choked to death on her own vomit. Police traced the telephone call to the barber's room at the nearby Marble Arch Hotel.

Late the next month, police put the barber under surveillance. In a single week, he was observed with four aboriginal women, all of whom he coaxed into dangerous states of intoxication.

Police listening outside hotel room doors overheard the barber encourage his victims. "Have a drink. Down the hatch, baby," he said. "Twenty bucks if you drink it right down."

He often offered cash for the chugging of hard liquor. Police intervened in all four cases. Two of the women had blood alcohol levels of 0.52 and 0.43.

He was convicted of manslaughter in Buckner's death. The judge said "alcohol was his deadly instrument of choice." The conviction was upheld on appeal, but he succeeded on another appeal in having his fifteen-year sentence reduced to nine.

"Neither that conviction, nor any of the deaths of the preceding six victims, were alleged by the Crown to be intentional acts,"

Justice Sam Toy wrote in reducing the sentence. "Although the appellant has left a trail of seven victims, the last was the first occasion when persons in authority in a forceful and realistic manner brought to the appellant's attention the fact that supplying substantial quantities of liquor to women who were prepared to drink with him was a contributing cause of their deaths for which he might be held criminally responsible."

In 2000, he tried again to change his name. The provincial government later closed a loophole allowing a criminal past to be masked through a simple name change.

Jordan's death in Victoria was announced in a thirty-two-word paid obituary notice that made no mention of his terrible crimes. His death was described as peaceful, unlike those of his victims.

The crimes inspired two notable works of fiction. The playwright Marie Clements wrote a well-received drama, *The Unnatural and Accidental Women*, giving voice to victims she felt had been overshadowed by the news media's unseemly interest in the killer's grotesque modus operandi. The case also provided the plot for the debut episodes of the award-winning CBC television series *Da Vinci's Inquest*.

August 8, 2006

ARTISTS

Sid Barron

CARTOONIST

(JUNE 13, 1917—APRIL 29, 2006)

Sid Barron's cartoons demanded more than a glance and a guffaw. His sly style lured readers into a lengthy examination of work rich in detail and wordy in execution. Diligent viewers would be well rewarded for their attention.

A typical Barron editorial cartoon included a scene that, at second glance, offered a cornucopia of visual puns, as well as such detritus as a cat holding a sign, or a biplane towing a banner.

These often included the two catchphrases that came to be associated with the artist—"Mild, isn't it?" and "Aren't the mountains pretty today?"

He poked fun at local foibles for the *Victoria Times* and *The Albertan* of Calgary. As well, his cartoons appeared in the *Toronto Star* for more than a quarter century. He often took as his subject the residents of the vast suburban expanses surrounding the downtown section of any large city. He renamed Don Mills, where he had once made his home, as Dawn Mills, a quiet, pretentious place where residents could not help but brag about the "exceptional quality" of their curbside trash.

His cartoons favoured gentle wit over biting satire. He did not usually take as his subject breaking news, or hapless politicians whose mistakes generated headlines. Instead, he found humour in the annoyances of everyday life. The critic Robert Fulford called him "the poet of the mundane."

In one cartoon, published by the *Star* in 1962, a disgruntled hockey fan watching his team on television has failed to notice the house burning down around him. A firefighter in the living room says, "Yeah, I'd have to go along on that . . . they're going to 'cheap penalty' themselves right out of the game." The slice-of-life setting, the overheard dialogue, and the absurdity of the situation are typical of events in what came to be called Barronland. He described the setting of his cartoons as Anyplace, Canada.

Barron shared the *Star's* editorial page with Duncan Macpherson, a brilliant caricaturist whose wit was as wicked as Barron's was dry. Macpherson skewered politicians with sometimes devastating results. It is said the reputation of former Prime Minister John Diefenbaker never recovered from his portrayal as a rabbit-toothed Marie Antoinette, which reduced a statesman to a figure of ridicule.

The pair gave the *Star* an enviable tag team, although not all readers were enamoured of Barron. One letter writer complained his works were "neither humorous nor meaningful but just nauseating." He had his defenders, too. "Macpherson's cartoons make us laugh at our leaders," another wrote, "but Barron's make us laugh at ourselves."

Sidney Arnold Barron was born in Toronto from a brief liaison between his young, unmarried mother and a Belgian officer billeted with his mother's family. From birth, he was raised by his aunt and her husband, and grew up knowing his biological mother as Auntie Daisy. The woman he called his mother was his aunt, Florence. He would be an adult before learning the truth.

He moved with his adoptive family to Victoria at the age of two. A shy, skinny boy, the usual childhood miseries were made the worse by a spectacular stammer. The impediment was so pronounced that in 1938 his father sent him to the National Hospital for Speech Disorders in New York. In later years, the cartoonist liked to tell a story about his return home to an anxious family. As they gathered around, he announced, "I'm c-c-c-c-cured!"

In the late 1930s, he took art lessons from Allan Edwards, a precocious talent who was two years younger than Barron and had followed him through South Park Elementary and Victoria High School. Another Edwards student was Pierre Berton, an ambitious writer who also entertained a desire to be a cartoonist. Barron found work illustrating window cards for Victoria shops, and later painting billboards in Toronto.

When wartime restrictions halted the importation of American comic books, a Canadian industry was born overnight. Barron found work as one of the freelancers in the stable of Educational Projects, a Montreal-based company whose bestselling title was *Canadian Heroes*. He was assigned to draw realistic depictions of historical events.

The *Star Weekly* magazine hired Barron as a freelance illustrator, a lucrative gig that ended when the publication began purchasing syndicated works from American artists. He then spent much of the 1950s seeking work on the West Coast and in Ontario.

"During this period, it later became apparent, he developed a caustic assessment of the manners and moral values of his compatriots who populated the newer suburbs of Canada's expanding cities," Peter Desbarats wrote in *The Hecklers*, a 1979 history of Canadian political cartooning.

Barron was hired as a cartoonist in 1958 by *Victoria Times* publisher Stuart Keate, who was eager for his afternoon daily to surpass the circulation of the morning rival, the *Colonist*. His works of gentle social commentary were entirely appropriate for the sleepy provincial capital. Three years later, Barron began selling cartoons to the *Star*.

In 1962, Barron moved to Calgary to work for *The Albertan*, all the while continuing with the *Star* as a client. Few of his Toronto readers knew his cartoons were drawn from so far away. The humorist Gary Lautens described the circumstance for *Star* readers in 1964. "Barron claims he is allergic to Toronto and every time he tries to live here (twice to date) he breaks out in airplane tickets and heads back for the foothills," he wrote.

Barron worked in black ink and crayon on commercial board, applying bits of toned laminate. His characters were saddled with Everyman names such as Ralph or, especially, Harold. In one cartoon, two women are leaning over a backyard fence and one says to the other: "Harold's a small 'l' liberal . . . he doesn't know whether to vote Conservative, Liberal, NDP or Socred."

The "puddy tat," a cynical feline with ridiculous stripes, would appear in a lower corner of panels holding a sign. Outdoor scenes would incorporate the biplane.

In 1983, editorial cartoonists met at a convention in Toronto, gathering one evening in the CN Tower restaurant high above the city. Roy Peterson, of the *Vancouver Sun*, hired an airplane to fly past while towing a banner reading, "Mild, isn't it?"

Barron was a gentle man of bohemian instinct, rarely lacking for female companionship, although a growing brood of children and stepchildren placed some limits on his romantic adventures. He met his third wife in Victoria in 1975 at what is now the Eric Martin Pavilion, where both were recuperating from mental breakdowns. Their union would last until Barron's death.

He quit drawing cartoons in 1989, retiring to Coombs on Vancouver Island. He and his artist wife painted, Barron indulging his passion for watercolour seascapes.

Several collections of his works were published over the years, including *Barron's Victoria* (1959), *2nd Annual Barron's Victoria* (1960), *Barron's Toronto* (1965), *Barron's Calgary Cartoons* (1967), *Barron Book (With Puddytat Centrefold)* (1972) and *The Best of Barron* (1985). He also illustrated the Eric Nicol humour book, *A Scar is Born* (1968).

The Art Gallery of Greater Victoria held an exhibition of his works in 1973. Barron cartoons that once hung in the home of BC Premier W.A.C. Bennett are part of a travelling exhibit from the Kelowna Museum.

The largest collection of his originals was gathered by the former

National Archives in Ottawa, now Library and Archives Canada, which has 1,344 drawings. The Glenbow Museum in Calgary owns seventy originals published in *The Albertan*.

At a memorial service in Victoria, mourners were invited to speak about the deceased. Some did so by quoting from memory the captions to decades-old cartoons.

May 15, 2006

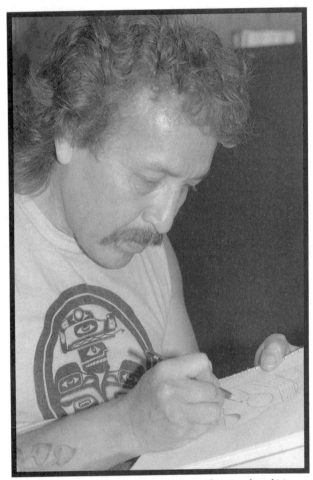

A carver and graphic artist of exceptional skill, Art Thompson's ambitious work can be found the world over. Here he sketches an outline at the Royal BC Museum's Thunderbird Park in 1987. IMAGE PN 17114 PROVIDED BY ROYAL BC MUSEUM, BC ARCHIVES

ART THOMPSON (TSA QWA SUPP)

CARVER

(DECEMBER 10, 1948—MARCH 30, 2003)

Art Thompson's bold works can be found in museums around the world: masks and rattles, bowls and poles, spoons and feast dishes. His free-flowing style reflected the traditional designs of the Nuu-chah-nulth people of Vancouver Island and his success helped revitalize a nearly defunct style.

He was a carver of profound skill, as well as a graphic artist whose designs bridged the centuries between an ancient culture and modern media. Perhaps his most reproduced image was the logo for the 1994 Commonwealth Games in Victoria.

The beauty captured in his art was all the more remarkable once the hellish details of his childhood became known through his testimony at a criminal trial and a later civil lawsuit. He had been raped as a child and regularly beaten at a residential school run by the United Church of Canada where, Thompson once said, "abuse was as predictable as daily prayer." The judge at the criminal trial praised Thompson for his eloquence, while the judge hearing the civil suit cited his courage.

Thompson lost many years to drug and alcohol addiction. He attempted suicide three times by his count. Making art provided an outlet from despair. The ability to rescue himself from so predictable a fate for a victim of sexual abuse fit well into his culture's myths of transformation. Thompson became a symbol for many Natives of the worthiness of giving witness to the insufferable acts they had endured.

Arthur Ivan Thompson was born in the village of Whyac on the Nitinaht reserve on southern Vancouver Island in 1948. The deprivations of his childhood began at age three when he was diagnosed with tuberculosis and sent to a hospital for Natives in Nanaimo, which would be his home for almost three years.

After his discharge, he lived with his mother's family in the Cowichan community of Koksilah. In 1955, he and two brothers were sent to the Alberni Indian Residential School, arriving in the baggage car of a train. On his first night, he wet his bed. His punishment the following morning was a strapping, which caused him to defecate in his pajamas. He was ordered to clean up the mess with his bare hands, he testified in 1999 at a civil suit heard by BC Supreme Court Justice Donald Brenner. At the time, he told court, he felt "terrified, lonesome, abandoned. There was no room for pity."

Students were barred from speaking their native languages, relying instead on their fragmentary knowledge of English. Thompson was addressed not by his name, but by his number, 511. He recalled life at the school as scary and punctuated with frequent corporal punishments administered by what he called sadistic adults. The most feared was dormitory supervisor Arthur Henry Plint, a Second World War veteran and predatory pedophile.

The boy frequently ran away, only to be returned to face further punishment. His only respite came in the summer months, when he spent time with his family. Among his fondest memories of those days were of watching his father and grandfather carve dugout canoes. After nine years at the residential school, Thompson fled for good when he was fourteen, finding work with a logging-survey crew. A back injury a few years later ended his work in the forests. At his lowest point, he was a heroin user stalking skid row.

In 1967, he enrolled in a commercial art program at Camosun

College on Vancouver Island, where he studied under Joe David and Ron Hamilton. Soon, Thompson began exploring the nearly forgotten forms of his own people, the Nuu-chah-nulth, who were known for a more free-flowing design, as well as the use of vibrant colours. He also took up carving and silversmithing. The common figures in his art came from Native myths of Wolf, Thunderbird, Whale, and Lightning Serpent. Thompson had been initiated when he was twelve into the Tl'uu Kwalaa (Wolf) Society, a traditional governing system. He inherited the name Tsa-qwa-supp from his father's family.

His works were bold and dramatic, and were sought by museums, embassies and private collectors around the world. He found a mass audience as a graphic artist, rendering logos for the Native relations department of BC Hydro and for the 1994 Commonwealth Games. He was one of three Native artists commissioned to design the Queen's Baton for the opening of the Games.

The medals he designed for the 1997 North American Aboriginal Games in Victoria depicted the creation story of the Dididaht people.

Two years earlier, Thompson had faced Arthur Plint, the former dormitory supervisor, in court. At a sentencing hearing in Port Alberni, Thompson donned a traditional headband and draped over his shoulders a ceremonial robe decorated by a thunderbird. He had paint applied to his face. In court, he delivered a thirty-minute account that left many spectators in tears.

"I want you to know I am a survivor," Thompson said, addressing Plint. "Look at these people. They are all around you, the survivors."

He told the court that his abuser's crimes made victims of uncounted others. "You tore apart communities with your acts. You installed a parental learning that was absolutely disgusting. All those learned habits I inflicted on my family, my people."

Plint pleaded guilty to sexually assaulting eighteen boys, ranging in age from six to thirteen, between 1948 and 1968. Three of his victims were forcefully sodomized. BC Supreme Court Justice

Douglas Hogarth sentenced the seventy-seven-year-old Plint, whom he called a "sexual terrorist," to an eleven-year sentence.

In 1999, Thompson testified during the hearing of a lawsuit he launched against the federal government, the United Church and four employees of the now-closed school. One of those employees was Plint. Thompson received compensation in an out-of-court settlement.

Thompson continued speaking on behalf of former residential-school students until his death at his Victoria home, aged fifty-four, four months after being diagnosed with cancer.

June 4, 2003

GERRY DEITER

PHOTOGRAPHER

(OCTOBER 20, 1934—DECEMBER 9, 2005)

The photographer Gerry Deiter attended all eight days of the 1969 Montreal bed-in for peace on the invitation of John Lennon and Yoko Ono. Deiter was on assignment for *Life* magazine, which did not publish the photographs after the story was bumped by the sudden death of Vietnamese leader Ho Chi Minh.

The images went unseen for more than three decades. Deiter decided to unearth his work in 2001 at his son's urging.

His photographs enjoyed widespread attention in recent years, in part because they offered a fuller document of that hectic bed-in week than had previously been available. The work was also remarkable for the intimacy with its subjects, who, despite days of intense scrutiny, were at ease with Deiter, in part because he had befriended Yoko Ono before she met the famous Beatle.

Deiter, a natural storyteller, amused acquaintances with anecdotes about his friendships with the artist Peter Max and the poet Allen Ginsberg. He claimed Jack Kerouac crashed on his living-room couch. Many assumed these to be apocryphal up to the point when Deiter provided photographic evidence.

Born in Brooklyn, New York, he borrowed his mother's camera at age twelve as a "ploy to gain popularity in school." A habitué of

Gerry Deiter learned photography in the army, then became a medical photographer before covering the fashion world. In the 1960s, he befriended the artist Peter Max, the poet Allen Ginsberg, and claimed Jack Kerouac used to crash on his living-room couch. In 1969, Life magazine assigned him to cover the bed-in for peace held in a Montreal hotel room by John Lennon and Yoko Ono. They asked him to stay the entire week. His photos of the memorable event remained unseen for nearly four decades. ESTATE OF GERRY DEITER, PHOTO COURTESY OF JOAN ATHEY

Ebbets Field, home of the Brooklyn Dodgers baseball team, Deiter considered himself an ambassador for the borough. "Growing up in Brooklyn prepares you to be just about anywhere in the world," he once told me.

During the Korean War, the US Army assigned the teenager to teach photography at military service clubs. He was later hired, at age twenty-one, to teach composition and darkroom techniques at the famed Pratt Institute in New York.

He also worked as a medical photographer, recording autopsies, as well as diseased organs. The macabre job taught him a great lesson about the human body: "How beautiful it was. How fragile it was." His skill led to assignments with New York's top fashion models, flesh of distinctly greater interest to the young man. He apprenticed with Francesco Scavullo and embraced a playboy's lifestyle, driving an Alfa Romeo sports car while squiring beauties to nightspots.

An interest in shooting jazz musicians led to Manhattan's art scene, which in turn led to an introduction to Ono, a Japanese avant-garde artist. A few years later, after Ono had taken up with Lennon, Deiter accompanied *Life* writer Charles Childs to Room 1742 at the Queen Elizabeth Hotel in Montreal, the assignment of a lifetime. Deiter was the only photojournalist to be in attendance for all eight days.

In a hectic week, he shot the couple and their visitors, including comedian Tommy Smothers, LSD guru Timothy Leary, and chanting, saffron-robed Hare Krishna acolytes. *Give Peace a Chance* was recorded amid the chaos and Deiter liked to think he could hear his own tenor singing harmony on the 1969 Apple Records release.

The photographs went unpublished, which Deiter later realized was a blessing as he got to retain copyright.

Deiter, who also handled assignments for the Canadian edition of *Time* magazine, enjoyed a peripatetic career. He travelled across Canada in a converted telephone van; sailed aboard a minesweeper racing to protest the testing of a nuclear bomb beneath Alaska's Amchitka Island; and in 1990 founded a muckraking newspaper in Prince Rupert. The weekly was launched in opposition to the Sterling-owned *Daily News*. Sterling, controlled by media baron Conrad Black, eventually bought the upstart rival and Deiter resigned.

"They turned my once-controversial and cutting-edge publication into an advertising rag and eventually shut it down, thereby achieving their objective of monopolizing the market," he wrote.

In recent years, Deiter lived aboard MV *Luigi*, a 1941 Matthews twin-engined cruiser docked in Victoria's Inner Harbour. In summer, he sailed the coast to document the remnants of the fishing and forestry industries.

The twenty-fifth anniversary of Lennon's death awakened interest in his life story, and the Deiter photographs were hailed as a welcome addition to the record. In his adopted city, the Royal British Columbia Museum displayed twenty-five of his photographs. At an event at the museum, Deiter joined Shaun Verreault of the band Wide Mouth Mason for a rousing rendition of "Give Peace a Chance." Deiter was heard on a live radio broadcast of the museum event and featured in television news coverage. He also appeared in a front-page photograph in the following day's edition of the *Victoria Times Colonist*. He died later that day, collapsing on a city street after suffering a heart attack.

After his death, at age seventy-one, friend Joan Athey gathered the bed-in photos in a book that received good notices. She also arranged for exhibitions of the photographs in Montreal and London, as well as at the Museum at Bethel Woods, near Woodstock, New York.

Deiter was bemused about the interest in the bed-in. "It's ironic as hell," he said. "I've been taking pictures since I was twelve years old. I finally get renown for one assignment I did for eight days thirty-six years ago."

December 12, 2005

John Di Castri

ARCHITECT

(JULY 26, 1924—SEPTEMBER 5, 2005)

John Di Castri brought to his staid Victoria hometown the architecture of flat roofs, glass walls and crisp horizontal lines. By combining stucco and concrete with such abundant natural materials as western hemlock and cedar shingles, he expressed a unique West Coast modernism.

He designed shops and churches, private houses and public buildings. His works dot the city, from Centennial Square downtown to the University of Victoria (UVic) campus in Gordon Head to private residences in the exclusive Uplands neighbourhood of Oak Bay.

Di Castri was an essential figure in West Coast architecture in the postwar years. He is also a rare one, whose name is promoted in the listings of real-estate agents.

Born and raised in a city named for a monarch, where architecture mimicked that found in the mother country, Di Castri rejected tradition for designs influenced by Frank Lloyd Wright. The public face of the Victoria of his childhood was dominated, then as now, by two massive buildings along the Inner Harbour: the neo-Romanesque legislative buildings and the baronial-and-chateau-style Empress Hotel, both by Francis Rattenbury. The best-known private

An innovative architect, Di Castri took chances in his work, bringing an eye-catching West Coast modernism to the schools, churches and funeral parlours he designed in his Victoria hometown. Many of his buildings have earned heritage designation from the city. PHOTO COURTESY OF SIMON DI CASTRI residences were grand Tudor Revival affairs from the pen of Samuel Maclure.

Di Castri eschewed the grand statement of such architecture for designs more respectful of setting. Forced to quit school at sixteen to find work, Di Castri was hired as an apprentice in the provincial department of public works. He loathed a job whose highlight turned out to be the delivery of mail to the provincial architect's office.

As he told it, an architect in the office noticed his keen interest in the drawings there and encouraged him to continue his education, which he did—by correspondence. At twenty-five, having worked briefly as a draftsman in the office of Birley Wade and Stockdill, he left Victoria to attend the University of Oklahoma. He studied under Bruce Goff at a time when the self-taught professor's career was at its most productive. The lessons learned from a mentor known for idiosyncratic design would inform his work for the rest of his career.

"One of the things we were taught was to create your own individual style," Di Castri told reporter Susan Down in 1997. "Design is basically a series of principles and they're timeless. They apply to any era. That way you don't have to be eclectic, you don't have to copy."

Di Castri returned to his hometown in 1951, entering into a brief partnership with F.W. Nichols. They designed a building for the Canadian Institute for the Blind in which curvilinear forms and a strong horizontal roofline were hints of what was to come from Di Castri. The building, at 1609 Blanshard Street, a major thoroughfare, echoes an unrealized residence by Goff. In recent years, it has housed a coffee shop, a McDonald's restaurant, and the offices of a weekly newspaper.

Opening his own practice in 1952, Di Castri established his reputation as an innovator two years later with his sensational Trend House at 3515 Richmond Avenue in suburban Saanich. One of ten model homes built across Canada to showcase BC lumber products, Di Castri's affordable design used plate glass and western hemlock. At just seventy-five square metres, the house was the smallest of the models.

The one-storey house boasted a dual roofline—a flat roof extends into the house with clerestory windows above. A large masonry chimney slices into the roof, giving the appearance of a bisected jet tail. On the side of the house away from the street, plate-glass windows extend from floor to ceiling, offering spectacular views of the Sooke Hills and snow-capped Olympic Mountains.

To those immune to the charms of the genre, it was a monstrosity looking like the crash site of a UFO.

It was "the most talked about house in BC," according to the newspapers, and the mayor opened the doors by cutting a red ribbon. The curious, who lined up by the thousands for a tour, were dazzled by an arrowhead-shaped floor plan.

The first resident of the Trend House was Gwen Cash, a pioneering woman reporter who wrote about the Doukhobors, the painter Emily Carr and the occultist known as Brother XII. As for those who did not appreciate the design, Cash said, "Like modern painting it was something that they couldn't understand." In 2009, the home was purchased by a couple who described themselves "as stewards of a remarkable piece of architecture."

Di Castri's private homes, including several of post-and-beam design tucked into the city's craggy rock outcroppings, were drawn only after he had several meetings with patrons. "Architecture is not a monument to the architect," he said. "A house that is worthy of the name of architecture should be satisfying on the inside and outside, both for the people living inside it and the people driving past who look at it." His signature included airy interiors, massive flagstone fireplaces and floor-to-ceiling plate-glass windows.

Along busy Fort Street, where one- and two-storey buildings were tarted up in faux Tudor trappings, Di Castri designed an office building to look like the walkup motels and apartments that filled the residential areas surrounding downtown. The result, called the Royal Trust Building in 1963, is remembered less for the architecture than for the mosaic murals covering the expansive windowless walls on the east and west side of the building's north face. The building, today a condominium project known as The Mosaic, remains a landmark on a street now promoted as Antique Row.

Among his other retail works are Ballantyne's Florist on Douglas Street, as well as the specialty shops and parkade on the north end of Centennial Square. The latter project was also completed in 1963, the same year the Student Union Building opened on UVic campus. His other university buildings include the Cornett Building (1966), with an exterior including shale, stucco, concrete, and local rock, and the cedar Interfaith Chapel (1985), using as its model the humble bungalow to create a nondenominational appearance.

He also designed schools and churches, including St. Joseph's, Sacred Heart and Christ the King. His design for Crystal Pool, a popular recreation facility, won an award from the US National Swimming Pool Foundation.

Much less successful, at least for critics, was a new entrance lobby opened in 1996 for the Royal BC Museum. The underwhelmed response of *Times Colonist* critic Robert Amos: "Basically, it's functional—hang up your coat, gather in groups, line up for tickets, ride up to the display floor." Robin Ward of the *Vancouver Sun* saw a "hand-me-down, postmodern monstrosity."

In 2002, the city granted heritage designation to a post-and-beam, three-level home at 1646 St. Francis Wood in the tony Rockland neighbourhood. The 1957 house offers spectacular views south across the Strait of Juan de Fuca and east to Mount Baker. The architect said the idea of the design was to have the house, which is nestled beside mature Garry oaks, "sitting on the rock, almost floating."

A retrospective of his art, writings and architecture was held in his hometown on the occasion of his eightieth birthday.

Di Castri's funeral mass was held at St. Patrick's Church, which Di Castri designed. As well, his remains were in the care of McCall Bros., for whom he designed a funeral home.

September 22, 2005

Politicians

Frank Howard nursed a secret during his long political career—he had served time in prison as a young man. After being blackmailed, he revealed his past to the public. He remained a popular politician and continued to advocate on behalf of the downtrodden. Howard also pushed for recognition of First Nations rights. He is shown here holding a miniature totem pole. PHOTO BY MARK VAN MANEN, PROVIDED BY THE *VANCOUVER SUN*

Frank Howard

EX-CONVICT ELECTED TO PARLIAMENT
(APRIL 27, 1925—MARCH 15, 2011)

Frank Howard went from breaking laws to making them.

Born into the most unpromising circumstance, he succumbed to the lure of crime before following a path that led to a seat in the House of Commons. The remarkable transformation is detailed in a memoir with a title succinctly capturing his life's journey—*From Prison to Parliament*. In it, he declares himself the only ex-convict to become a Canadian lawmaker. Indeed, it is easier to imagine a reverse trajectory.

Howard became a champion of working people and a tribune for society's least favoured members, from aboriginals to prisoners forgotten behind penitentiary walls. In his long career as a Member of Parliament, he took part in a three-year filibuster that led to reform of the divorce laws. He is also credited with helping those who lived on reserves gain universal adult suffrage in 1960.

A miner and logger before he ran for office, he campaigned by scaling poles at sporting events and by reeling in ling cod the size of a child. For seventeen years he represented an isolated and far-flung constituency in northwestern British Columbia encompassing a territory nearly the size of France, but with a fraction of the people.

With a craggy face topped by a shock of hair and chevron-shaped eyebrows, which turned white in old age—lending him the air of an Old Testament prophet—it was no stretch to imagine the solid six-footer as a lumberjack. The Native Brotherhood of BC bestowed on him the name Weget, a Gitga'at honour meaning big, or powerful.

As a teenager, he had occasion to search for his birth certificate. He knew he had been placed with another family shortly after his birth, but not until he dug into the archives did he discover how confused was his biography.

"Here I am with two different surnames and four different birth dates," he wrote in his memoir. "Who the hell am I?"

Frank Robert Howard was born in Kimberley on or about April 27, 1925. His mother, Dorothy Naas, worked as a prostitute on the outskirts of the mining town in the Kootenay River Valley. His father, Rowlat Widlake Steeves, is believed to have been her pimp. On his birth, he was given to foster parents who later spoke unkindly of the birth parents. They were described with contempt as "unmarried, no-good, rotten sons of bitches."

While in grade school, Howard scavenged beer bottles, their return to the brewery bringing a penny each, which he then used to buy single cigarettes to smoke with friends. Daily life involved misadventures and petty thievery. After he and two pint-sized scofflaws stole a butterscotch pie from the kitchen window of the Sullivan Hotel, he was taken before a judge, who determined he was a neglected child. At twelve, he was sent away from the only family he had known. On the journey to an orphanage in Vancouver, a policeman escorting the boy molested him as he cried on a bed in a motel room.

A docile, quiet child, Howard endured a stint at the Alexandra Children's Home on West Seventh Avenue—"a warehouse containing kids in institutional clothing," he would write—before being directed to the first of a series of foster homes. He contemplated suicide and ran away several times, once hot-wiring a stolen automobile in a desperate bid to return to Kimberley to visit his foster brother.

Before he dropped out in Grade 10, Howard worked after school and in the summer in a foundry, pouring molten iron into moulds for $4 a week.

He found a wartime job in the Vancouver shipyards, but, with an accomplice, went on a month-long crime spree in the summer of 1943, robbing two jewellery stores and the Castle Hotel while armed with a revolver. In one of the holdups, the pair netted $2,000 in rings, watches and diamonds after sticking a gun in the back of an elderly employee.

Howard was convicted of three counts of armed robbery and sentenced to two years on each charge. He recalled anxiously awaiting the judge's final verdict. "I remember listening for those words, either 'consecutive' or 'concurrent.' I was lucky. The word was 'concurrent.'" He served twenty months in the federal penitentiary in New Westminster, with time off for good behaviour, before being released on May 1, 1945. He walked out with $10 in his pocket and a prison-bought suit on his back.

A criminal record made it difficult to find work, so he abandoned his foster name—he had been convicted as Frank Thomas Woodd—and became Frank Howard. He found jobs as a logger, and after less than four years on the job became an organizer for the International Woodworkers of America, serving as president of Local 1-71 for seven years.

He stood as a Co-operative Commonwealth Federation candidate in the 1952 provincial election, challenging a Coalition cabinet minister in Skeena. "I wasn't attracted to the CCF because of any theories it held regarding sociopolitical matters," he wrote. "I joined because I was a trade unionist; because corporations had the ear of government and workers did not."

He lost, but claimed a seat in the legislature in Victoria the following year by a 13-vote margin. After a single term, he lost to a Social Credit rival by 63 votes.

He then set his sights on Ottawa, defeating Liberal incumbent Ted Applewhaite, an insurance salesman, in the federal riding of Skeena in 1957. Howard would represent Skeena for seventeen years, withstanding both the John Diefenbaker sweep of 1958 and Trudeaumania a decade later. Howard held the seat for the CCF and its successor, the New Democratic Party, for seven campaigns before losing in 1974 to the Liberals' Iona Campagnolo, a future Lieutenant-Governor of British Columbia.

A fierce advocate for his constituents, Howard once wrote to the provincial highways minister to complain about the state of the unpaved road between Williams Lake and Bella Coola. He told Philip Gaglardi, a politician who drove so fast he was known as Flyin' Phil, that the three graders on the highway were known as High Blade, Never-Scratch and Old Feather Touch.

"The road is pimpled and warted with rocks," Howard wrote. "There are sharp rocks, spiked rocks, rugged, jagged and craggy rocks. They are round, square, conical, oval, notched, toothed and spired. There are large rocks, medium-sized rocks and even some pebbles. They protrude, project, pout, bulge and bunch themselves from all parts of the road. Between the rocks there are cavities, con-cavities, indentations, craters, sockets, depressions, hollows, dips, pits, troughs, basins, washboards, and holes of all sorts."

The monthly mimeographed newsletter he mailed to eighteen hundred constituents once sandwiched a recipe for chocolate cake between news of the latest political developments in Ottawa. The politician advocated cooking as a hobby for men, comparing it to bowling as a way to relax after work.

A blunt, outspoken figure in the House, he received rebukes from the Speaker more than once. He delighted in sniping with Conservatives. Howard worked with caucus mate Arnold Peters to block eleven hundred divorce petitions from Quebec and Newfoundland, two provinces whose lack of divorce courts left the matter to Parliament. The pair filibustered for three years to draw attention to the need for reform of Canada's archaic divorce laws.

Speaking in the House in 1964, Howard warned that Quebec's demands would be insatiable and suggested the rest of Canada should proceed on the notion that someday the Confederation would consist of only nine provinces. At least one member of the

NDP caucus later told the House they challenged Howard's vision of the future.

Howard gained a reputation as an advocate for penal reform, denouncing the "deplorable conditions" at St. Vincent de Paul Penitentiary at Montreal. Few knew his advocacy came from personal experience. The parliamentarian confided his criminal past to party leaders and close friends, but the public remained ignorant until he made a televised confession in 1967.

After receiving an extortion note, which he shared with police, Howard purchased airtime on CFTK-TV in Terrace. He admitted to having spent time in jail, though he refused to offer details of his crimes, which were later revealed by reporters who checked legal records. The admission was big news, in part because of the dramatic circumstance. The *Vancouver Sun*'s front-page headline read, "MP Frank Howard admits: I served time in penitentiary."

Howard had received a note demanding a payment of $5,000 in bills of $10, $20 and $50. This was to be sent in a small box wrapped in brown paper addressed to a fictitious name in care of general delivery at the Vancouver post office. The blackmailer promised to repay the money at $100 per week for one year.

"If not," the note threatened, "I will totally ruin you by distributing proof of your past to your friends, relatives, political associates and appropriate authorities." It was signed, "An old friend."

Gary Stephen Ross, the eighteen-year-old son of a union organizer and Howard family friend, pleaded guilty to the extortion attempt. Howard called for leniency. Ross received a one-year jail term, which was reduced on appeal to a two-year suspended sentence. The youth went on to a distinguished career as an author and publisher. He said he had a reconciliation with Howard.

The exposé gained Howard sympathy, not censure.

His advocacy on behalf of Native people included harsh criticism of a bureaucracy he saw enriching itself at the expense of his constituents. "We should have a bonfire and burn the Indian Act," he said in 1969. "There's a group of empire builders in the department that seeks to perpetuate themselves." The walls of his Ottawa office were decorated with his own paintings of the totem poles to be found back home.

In 1971, Howard entered the federal NDP leadership contest called after the retirement of T.C. (Tommy) Douglas. He launched his candidacy with harsh words against a radical wing of the party known as the Waffle, whose call for the nationalization of resource industries he decried as politically naive and lacking common sense. A low-key campaign seemed based on the gamble of winning delegates at the convention in Ottawa. Shortly before the vote, Howard spent a fortnight touring the Antipodes with Jean Chrétien, then Indian Affairs and Northern Development minister. On the first ballot, Howard got just 124 votes of 1,698 cast, finishing last of five candidates in a race won on the fourth ballot by David Lewis. Among the defeated challengers was future party leader Ed Broadbent.

After losing his seat, Howard worked briefly as a consultant on aboriginal affairs for Dave Barrett's NDP government in British Columbia. He later became a stockbroker with Richardson Securities of Canada.

Howard re-entered the political fray in his home province in 1979, knocking off stalwart Socred MLA Cyril Shelford, a rancher known as the "Maverick of the North." Howard won re-election four years later before being defeated in 1986.

He retired to Surrey, outside Vancouver, where he lived with his third wife, Joane Humphrey, a journalist known professionally as J.J. McColl. A first marriage, to Edith Horvath, ended in divorce, while a second marriage, to Julie Peacock, ended with her death from cancer in 1999. The late-in-life romance with Ms. Humphrey—the bride was sixty-five, the groom seventy-seven when they enjoyed a June wedding in 2002—animated the couple, who remained devoted to one another until her death six years later from amyotrophic lateral sclerosis (Lou Gehrig's disease).

A baker of prized Christmas fruitcakes, Howard also enjoyed gardening and photography. He wrote the draft of a science-fiction novel and was designing a board game based on politics at the time of his death.

Like many who make a grievous mistake when young, he was haunted throughout his life by his past.

"I'm grateful to the general public for its acceptance of the fact that a teenage blunder can be overcome and forgiven," he wrote. "But the blunderer must continue to prove to himself, and therefore to others, that overcoming the blunder is permanent."

June 24, 2011

*A maverick politician of outspoken opinion, Jack Kempf spent many years on the
Social Credit backbenches before being named to cabinet. He lasted only a few
months before being fired for travel expense irregularities. This 1999 photo shows
him outside a courtroom where he testified against former Premier Bill Vander
Zalm—the man who ousted him from cabinet.* PHOTO BY MARK VAN MANEN,
PROVIDED BY THE *VANCOUVER SUN*

JACK KEMPF

WOLFMAN JACK

(MAY 12, 1935—JULY 1, 2003)

Jack Kempf was a maverick politician from northern British Columbia who earned the nickname "Wolfman Jack" for his ardent support of a wolf kill. Kempf had a sixteen-year career as a provincial MLA to which the description "colourful" hardly does justice.

A large man with a booming voice and no fear of using it, Kempf was a blustery and pompous figure whose malapropisms added a touch of buffoonery to his reputation. He once called a Social Credit colleague an "idiot" and blamed his party's policies for ruining prime farmland. He once described legal aid as a socialist invention foisted upon the taxpayers by the NDP, only to be reminded that his own party had approved the financing of the program.

He portrayed himself as the protector of the little guy, especially of small logging operators, and complained that only his outspoken behaviour kept him from his rightful place in cabinet.

When he finally was appointed to cabinet, he lasted a few months before being fired by Premier Bill Vander Zalm.

He was dismissed as forests minister in 1987 for improprieties involving his travel expenses while a parliamentary secretary. He stewed over his treatment, as the premier had not waited for an official investigation of his actions.

The locks were changed on the ministry offices and security guards were ordered to bar Kempf. Later, the provincial comptroller-general said Kempf had acted improperly, although no criminal charges were laid. Among Kempf's mistakes was using travel points accumulated while on government business to cover the cost of his wife's flight to Ottawa.

The hint of wrongdoing enraged Kempf. "I pay every bloody penny for her," he told reporters. "It cost me $3,000 just to take her to China. I even pay the differential rate if I stay in a hotel where there's a different single and double rate. That's how meticulous I am."

Kempf alleged he was a victim of a conspiracy hatched by the premier and the major forest companies. He also accused the Attorney General of having his telephones wiretapped.

He quit the Social Credit caucus to sit as an independent, rejoining the party in time for the next election campaign in 1991, during which it was revealed that he faced criminal charges over the improper use of constituency funds.

The news was a blow to the re-election chances of new Social Credit Premier Rita Johnston, who days earlier had been forced to disavow the candidacy of a Socred who turned out to be a Nazi sympathizer. Reporters helpfully suggested the premier's memoir of the campaign be titled *Mein Kempf*.

Kempf refused to step down as a Social Credit candidate. When the premier ordered another nomination meeting, Kempf's campaign manager won the contest only to refuse to file papers.

No Socred appeared on the ballot in the riding of Bulkley Valley–Stikine. Kempf ran as an independent, finishing third.

Five months later, he pleaded guilty to breach of trust in provincial court. He had used his constituency allowance to lease a mobile home as a constituency office. He subsequently used the vehicle as security to repay a personal loan.

A special prosecutor called for a jail term, but Judge Edmond

Cronin instead fined the former minister $11,000 and placed him on one year's probation.

Kempf's lawyer acknowledged his client was cloaked in "the dark reality of public scorn."

"If I've erred, I'm sorry," Kempf said outside the court.

After his conviction, Kempf left British Columbia for a new life in Loreto, on the eastern shore of Mexico's Baja Peninsula. There, he indulged his passion for fishing.

Jack Joseph Kempf, who was born in Kelowna, graduated from Similkameen High School in Keremeos, a village in the midst of Okanagan fruit orchards.

He began working at the Buck River Lumber Co. in Houston, BC, in 1958, rising to logging superintendent. In 1968, the company was bought out by Bowater-Bathurst, whose Bulkley Valley Forest Industries said it planned to create the largest integrated forests complex in Canada. Instead, it sold the Houston operation and many employees were laid off.

In 1971, Kempf bought the Pleasant Valley Restaurant, became active in the local chamber of commerce and was elected a district alderman before winning the first of two terms as mayor of Houston (population 2,500) in 1974.

He handily won election to the provincial legislature the following year as the Social Credit MLA for Omineca, a sparsely populated riding of forests and mountains. He would be re-elected in three subsequent elections, never getting less than 55 percent of the vote.

Premier Bill Bennett ended Kempf's eleven-year exile on the backbenches by naming him Lands, Parks and Housing Minister in 1986 as part of a "political renewal" shuffle. Kempf was almost immediately criticized when it was discovered he was living in a subsidized co-operative project in Victoria, paying only $476 a month for a three-bedroom townhouse. His salary as a minister was $71,000. He soon moved.

As a backbencher in 1984, Kempf had written a letter to the editor calling for a raise for MLAs. "Never would I ever suggest that a provincially elected representative should get rich on his or her pay," he wrote, "but I do believe they should at least break even and at least be able to live as third-class citizens."

September 18, 2003

DAVE STUPICH

BINGOGATE FRAUDSTER

(DECEMBER 5, 1921—FEBRUARY 8, 2006)

Dave Stupich masterminded a fraud that brought down an NDP premier and sullied the reputation of a party to which he had dedicated much of his life. Stupich's crimes stand out for their jaw-dropping audacity. For many years, money from bingo games was illegally funnelled to accounts he controlled. About $1 million was diverted in a complex and labyrinthine series of transactions. The NDP benefited from the slush fund, as did Stupich himself.

The scandal, which became known as Bingogate, shocked many among the party faithful. A stalwart member of a party supposedly devoted to defending the powerless was exposed as stealing from charities.

Premier Mike Harcourt resigned in the wake of the revelations, though he was not implicated in the schemes.

In 1999, Stupich pleaded guilty to criminal charges of fraud and running an illegal lottery scheme. He was sentenced to house arrest with electronic monitoring for two years less a day. The judge who imposed the sentence on the former politician, then aged seventy-seven, said he was lenient owing to Stupich's ill health. The broken and disgraced politician was showing early signs of dementia.

Shortly after the sentencing, Harcourt described his onetime

Dave Stupich ended his long political career in disgrace while at the centre of the Bingogate scandal. Stupich cut a dejected figure under questioning in 1999 by Lyndsay Smith, commission counsel for a public inquiry into the scandal. PHOTO BY GLENN BAGLO, PROVIDED BY THE *VANCOUVER SUN*

ally's behaviour as "the longtime, clever and calculating actions of an embezzler and a liar." The former premier, whose political career had ended under a shadow, said those actions "smeared a number of totally innocent people, myself included." Harcourt had once been assured by Stupich that the fuss over the bingo money was "a bunch of nothing."

A man of dignified bearing, Stupich represented the working-class city of Nanaimo in the BC legislature in Victoria and the House of Commons in Ottawa.

In a party with a poor reputation for financial acumen, the chartered accountant's agility with numbers made him a member whose talents were touted to business and to reporters. He served in the 1970s as BC's finance minister and agriculture minister. He was provincial party president and headed the NDP caucus in Ottawa. He entertained aspirations about becoming NDP leader in BC, although it turned out he thought better of his attributes than did party delegates.

He also had an earlier brush with the courtroom in his political career. Social Credit Premier Bill Bennett told a reporter he replaced night sessions of the legislature for morning sessions "because MLAs don't pour scotch on their cornflakes." Stupich took the statement as an attack on the NDP Opposition. In a newsletter to constituents, Stupich wrote that the premier's drinking habits left him unfit for evening sittings.

The premier sued for libel, winning $10,000 in damages and court costs at a trial where the customary courtroom decorum was replaced by the argumentative belligerence of Question Period. In fact, Stupich's lawyer was Alex Macdonald, a long-time friend and former Attorney General.

A final twist to what became known as the "scotch-and-cornflakes" case came when Stupich tried to pay the award with 1,667 shares of BC Resources Investment Corporation, a company created by the premier from provincial assets. Stupich said he had paid $6 each for the shares, for a total of $10,002. They were then trading at about $3.15 each. Bennett refused to accept the shares and walked across the floor of the legislature to return them. Stupich later issued a cheque to cover the award.

David Daniel Stupich was born in Nanaimo and raised in nearby South Wellington, a former mining town. After completing high school, he joined the Royal Canadian Air Force, serving as a pilot and flight instructor during the Second World War. After the war, he enrolled at the University of British Columbia, where he studied poultry husbandry before graduating with a degree in agriculture in 1949.

He first ran for the provincial legislature that same year, carrying the Co-operative Commonwealth Federation banner in Nanaimo and The Islands. He lost to George Pearson of the coalition formed by Liberals and Progressive Conservatives to prevent the Co-operative Commonwealth Federation (CCF) from attaining power.

Stupich ran again in 1952, as the province experimented with a preferential ballot. The new voting method would cost him a seat and his party a chance at power. He led with 3,715 votes after the first count, followed by Lorenzo (Larry) Giovando of the Conservatives with 3,346. By the fourth and final count, after secondary and tertiary choices of the eliminated candidates were distributed, the Conservative at last emerged victorious. After many weeks of confusion, W.A.C. Bennett of the Social Credit convinced the Lieutenant-Governor to allow his party to form the government, having won nineteen seats to the CCF's eighteen. The Liberals had six seats and the Conservatives four, while one independent was elected.

Had Stupich taken Nanaimo, Bennett's claim on the premier's post would have been much weaker, as the CCF had outpolled the upstart Socreds.

The province returned to the polls the following year. Once again, Stupich led after the first count, followed by a Liberal, with the incumbent Conservative in third place, and two other candidates trailing. On the fifth count, the Conservative hung onto the seat by just 18 votes.

It was in the aftermath of those two bitter defeats that Stupich founded the Nanaimo Commonwealth Holding Society (NCHS) in 1954. The new group was to sell bonds to finance the opening of a meeting hall, an important step for the party at a time when many commercial owners refused to rent space to socialists. Over time, the society operated as a fundraising arm of the CCF and its successor, the New Democratic Party.

The society bought its first bingo machine in 1959. Nanaimo became a hotbed of bingo-parlour socialists.

Stupich at last won a seat in the legislature in the 1963 general election, defeating a Social Credit challenger by just 19 votes. (The province had returned to a first-past-the-post system.) He enjoyed a relative landslide with a 45-vote victory to win re-election three years later.

In 1969, he lost the seat to Frank Ney, the swashbuckling mayor of Nanaimo whose habit it was to dress in a pirate costume to promote the city's annual bathtub race across Georgia Strait to Vancouver.

Stupich reclaimed the seat during the NDP's 1972 breakthrough, in which the party won power after almost four decades in Opposition. Premier Dave Barrett rewarded long-time loyalists with cabinet seats. Stupich's brief stint in power included the creation of the Agricultural Land Reserve in 1973. The reserve protected farmlands under pressure for development. The fertile Fraser Valley east of Vancouver was especially threatened. About 4.7-million hectares, roughly 5 percent of the province, was placed in the reserve. The act was angrily contested by landowners whose property values dropped, yet the reserve continued under succeeding Socred and Liberal administrations.

Stupich survived his party's defeat in 1975, becoming Opposition Finance Critic. He won re-election in 1979, 1983 and 1986.

A candidacy to replace Barrett ended after the third ballot at a leadership convention in Vancouver in 1984. Stupich had only 114 votes, trailing David Vickers (339), Bob Skelly (313) and Bill King (292). In defeat, he eschewed a chance to play kingmaker, refusing to endorse any of his opponents. "I was the best candidate," he said, "and I don't believe in recommending second best."

In the end, Skelly won, only to be defeated in the next general election by the charismatic Bill Vander Zalm.

In 1988, Stupich decided to contest the NDP nomination for the federal riding of Nanaimo–Cowichan. He defeated Ted Miller, a former MP whose supporters felt he had a claim on the riding. Stupich served a five-year term in Ottawa.

The animosity generated in the nomination showdown would later find expression in revelations about the financial sleight of hand being conducted at the NCHS. The society had financed the construction of a hotel and a six-storey office building, which was jokingly called Red Square. Rising interest rates left the society about $2 million in debt. Money from bingo games, which should have been distributed to the poor and the disabled, among others, was instead diverted to society coffers.

Rumours of wrongdoing had been rife for years and the RCMP launched criminal investigations in 1979 and 1988 without charges being laid.

Further revelations in the early 1990s, including reports by the *Vancouver Sun* and the decision of charities to withdraw from bingo games held at Red Square, preceded the appointment of a special Crown prosecutor.

The prosecutor's report implicated the NCHS and three related societies, which faced fourteen criminal charges for misappropriation of funds. The societies pleaded guilty, were fined $55,000 and ordered to pay $100,000 in restitution to charities. Stupich said three of the societies had no assets and had no intention of paying the fine.

The continued outcry over the money led Premier Harcourt to order a forensic audit of the NCHS. Stupich refused to co-operate, successfully petitioning the BC Supreme Court in his resistance to provide documents that could include personal records. His court success was a pyrrhic victory.

The report by auditor Ron Parks painted a damning portrait.

Parks concluded that Stupich made "significant unauthorized loans to himself" from the society's accounts and had personally benefited by as much as $374,000 by "manipulating the financial records of NCHS and related societies."

After reading the report, Premier Harcourt said he felt physically ill. "The NDP, through the NCHS, had at one time benefited from picking the pockets of the penniless, the handicapped and the indigent," he wrote in a 1996 memoir.

The report's imminent release to the public, including a media contingent anticipating revelations shocking even by British Columbia standards, was halted by the start of a criminal investigation. The delay further wounded the reputations of prominent NDPers, foremost among them the premier, who had already decided to resign.

On October 12, 1995, the RCMP raided NDP headquarters and Stupich's home on Gabriola Island, as well as five other locations. The Parks report was ordered released the next day by a justice of the BC Supreme Court.

The audit was filled with revelations embarrassing to the NDP, including details of kickback schemes involving charities, as well as the collection of anonymous corporate donations in violation of the party's constitution. More than $50,000 had been illegally funnelled to the party's newspaper. Someone identified only by the initials "D.B." had deposited an unexplained $12,500 in $50 notes to the NCHS account. Barrett later told a provincial inquiry that the money had been contributed by an anonymous donor.

The NDP used the NCHS account as a bank and a slush fund, according to the audit.

In 1998, the RCMP laid charges against Stupich, his partner Elizabeth Marlow, his daughter Marjorie Boggis, NDP Provincial Secretary Joseph Denofrio, and the party's newspaper company. The charges against Marlow, Boggis and Denofrio were stayed the following June when Stupich pleaded guilty. He avoided jail but was unable to spend his house arrest in his customary comfort on Gabriola Island. Instead, the judge ordered Stupich to live at a daughter's more modest residence in Nanaimo.

February 16, 2006

WRITERS

JACK WINTER

COMEDY SCREENWRITER

(FEBRUARY 9, 1942—DECEMBER 29, 2006)

As a television writer, Jack Winter sent Fonzie to a psychiatrist; got Felix and Oscar to make up after squabbling; and helped the Monkees escape romantic entanglements.

Winter's credits include some of the most successful situation comedies in television history. He wrote episodes of *The Dick Van Dyke Show*, *The Mary Tyler Moore Show* and *The Odd Couple*, as well as the *Happy Days* spinoff *Laverne and Shirley*. He also enjoyed lucrative work as a movie script doctor, helping to make a success of the 1988 Tom Hanks comedy *Big*.

In 2001, Winter married Ekram Fadlelmola, known as Moon, a Sudanese woman he had met at the airport in Kathmandu several years earlier. She had so enjoyed her time as a student at the University of Victoria they decided to settle in the British Columbia capital. He sold his Manhattan apartment to buy a leafy property in suburban Saanich, which included a pond that he stocked with frogs, a boyhood passion. By then, Winter was all but immobilized by chronic back pain that spinal fusions and surgeries failed to ease. Though horizontal, he wrote and self-published a comic memoir, *The Answer to Everything*, which he sold online for $13 US.

Winter was born in New York City to the violinist Paul Winter and the former Margaret Klein, a model, painter and buyer for a department store. The elder Winter had been a child prodigy, who at age twenty-three in 1937 became the youngest member of the NBC Symphony Orchestra under the conductor Arturo Toscanini. He performed in live radio broadcasts, as well as for studio audiences in the early days of television. He often brought his son to the studio.

In his memoir, Jack Winter includes an account of hanging around the set of *Your Show of Shows* with Sid Caesar and Imogene Coca, where he recalled an atmosphere like a "comedy circus." The boy eavesdropped on conversations, as though auditing a course in comedy writing. His experiences with the show's wisecracking writers, a roster including Neil Simon, Mel Brooks and Woody Allen, prepared him for a quick recovery when he once accidentally interrupted his parents' lovemaking. "I quickly sized up the situation," he wrote, "then leaned on my elbow against the doorjamb and said, very matter-of-factly, 'Can I have a raise in my allowance?'"

At university, he majored in philosophy and minored in the *Harvard Lampoon*, the student-produced humour magazine. Winter was editor-in-chief when the fashion magazine *Mademoiselle* hired the *Lampoon* staff in 1961 to produce a parody to run in place of the July edition, a notoriously poor seller. The production of the parody caught the fancy of the *New York Times*, which dispatched a reporter to follow the writers, models and photographers for a day, including a shoot involving a wrestler. One of the spreads was headlined "Clothes to be Caught Dead In."

For his part, Winter was unimpressed by the fashions selected by the magazine's regular editors. "Frankly, the colours on these clothes are too bold and bright," he told the *Times*. "I thought clothes were meant to flatter a woman, not distract from her face."

The parody was a newsstand sensation, owing perhaps to a striking cover image of a comely model with a fly on her nose. Winter said a double press run—1.3 million issues—sold out within a week. A fake advertisement for a fat-removing cream solicited five thousand responses.

Among those on the *Lampoon* staff with him were Christopher Cerf, who would win Grammys and Emmys for songwriting, and John Berendt, author of the best-selling book *Midnight in the Garden of Good and Evil.*

Winter notes in his memoir that he was the second-youngest member of Harvard '62. The youngest was Theodore Kaczynski, who went on to earn notoriety—and a life sentence—as the Unabomber.

After graduation, Winter travelled to Miami Beach, Florida, to join the writing staff for a show starring Jackie Gleason, the singing funny man with a notorious reputation for mistreating employees. He did not stay long.

Soon after, Winter was writing for *The Tonight Show* on a night when guest host Bill Cosby was to interview a frog puppet named Kermit. Since the Muppets were still unfamiliar to a national audience, Cosby instructed the show's writers to dress his amphibious guest in a trench coat as though he were a spy like James Bond. During the live taping, the host asked the frog if he had a licence to kill. "No," Kermit replied, "but I have a learner's permit to hurt." The studio audience's raucous laughter segued into a standing ovation. The salute inspired the producer to end the segment a minute early by cutting to commercial.

Winter was distraught. "How could you do that? You cut out the ending."

Cosby then gave him some advice he never forgot in a long career of writing. "Kid, if you get a laugh like that, it is an ending—because you'll never be able to top it."

The first full script Winter prepared as a sitcom writer won a coveted Writers Guild of America award. In a *Dick Van Dyke Show* episode titled "You Ought to Be in Pictures" the show's star, playing a television comedy writer named Rob Petrie, is directed to kiss a voluptuous Italian starlet for a low-budget foreign film. Bumbling and stammering, he makes sure to first get his hovering wife's permission with a plaintive, "M-May I?"

The prize allowed Winter the luxury of writing a stage play in

New York, from where he would dash to Hollywood to crank out a television script whenever funds ran low. In 1967, he wrote five episodes of *The Monkees*, a series about the madcap adventures of four musicians whose naivety constantly put them at odds with both star-struck female fans and men in suits with less than idealistic motives. In one episode ("Monkee Mayor"), Winter had Michael Nesmith run for political office. He followed with contributions to *Love, American Style* and an episode of *The Mary Tyler Moore Show* in which an ambitious consultant upsets the staff at WJM-TV.

For *The Odd Couple*, Winter wrote a line for uncouth sportswriter Oscar Madison, played by Jack Klugman, who defends his use of a condiment on salad. "I like ketchup," he says. "It's like tomato wine." Winter also directed several episodes of the hit series.

Not all his assignments were as successful. He wrote for the forgettable *Getting Together*, a 1971 Bobby Sherman vehicle owing more than a little to *The Partridge Family*, which was inspired in turn by the real-life Cowsill singing family. The 1976 series *Sirota's Court* received favourable notice from the *Times* but lasted only two seasons. The audiences were larger for his scripts for *Happy Days* and *Laverne and Shirley*.

A rare movie credit included citation as special adviser on *Big*. Winter earned $5,000 per day as a script doctor, high-paying work that he found "too irregular, too artistically unsatisfying, and much too stressful."

Winter dated the actresses Diane Keaton and Joyce Jillson, whose modest Broadway and Hollywood career was superseded by her success as a syndicated astrologer. He also once had a blind date with Candice Bergen, although he thought her too humourless to call for a second date. His friends thought him crazy.

More long lasting was his relationship with retired basketball great Earl (The Pearl) Monroe, with whom he played a weekly game of tennis. Though not a braggart by nature, Winter could be induced to tell the story about the time he defeated tennis champion Pete Sampras. Winter was writing an article for *Sports Illustrated* and only managed a narrow victory through a series of fortunate circumstances. Also a factor was that his opponent was aged nine at the time.

Winter spent many thousands of hours labouring over a stage play that was never produced. To augment his income, he imported and sold antique Turkish tapestries known as kilim. He sold many to his friends in show business. The actress and writer, Carrie Fisher, once referred to him on television as "my friend, Jack Winter, a writer and rug dealer." Winter later wrote, "Since she was known for having a substance-abuse problem, viewers thought she'd said 'writer and *drug* dealer.' Several people who knew me didn't know about my rug business, but they knew that I never earned any money from the play—and they couldn't help wondering."

Winter was responsible for the celebrated comic essay, "How I Met My Wife," published by *The New Yorker* in 1994. "I was furling my wieldy umbrella for the coat check when I saw her standing alone in a corner," he wrote. "She was a descript person, a woman in a state of total array. Her hair was kempt, her clothing shevelled, and she moved in a gainly way. I wanted desperately to meet her, but I knew I'd have to make bones about it since I was travelling cognito."

January 22, 2007

The prolific humourist Eric Nicol wrote forty-one books and more than six-thousand newspaper columns during a celebrated career that saw him win the Leacock award for humour three times. Among his books were such titles as, A Scar is Born, Skiing is Believing, and Canada: Cancelled Because of Lack of Interest. His memoir was titled, appropriately, Anything for a Laugh. PHOTO COURTESY OF THE ESTATE OF ERIC NICOL

ERIC NICOL

HUMOURIST

(DECEMBER 28, 1919—FEBRUARY 2, 2011)

The wordsmith Eric Nicol delighted, bemused and titillated readers with a prolific outpouring of light essays.

Nicol wrote radio plays and stage comedies, gaining a national audience with forty-one books, the last of these published by the nonagenarian a year before his death. The title carries a typical Nicol pun: *Script Tease*.

In a seven-year span, three of Nicol's volumes—*The Roving I* (1951), *Shall We Join the Ladies?* (1956) and *Girdle Me a Globe* (1958)—won Stephen Leacock Memorial Medals for Humour.

A shy man who was as witty in person as on the page, he claimed not to smoke or drink or chase women—but looked forward to doing so once the royalties began rolling in.

Celebrated by critics, he felt his readers regarded humour as "a low calling."

"In the eyes of Canadians," he wrote, "writing humour is like an illicit love affair: It is excusable provided you don't make a habit of it, or accept payment for what you have done."

Much of his prodigious output first saw publication in newspapers, including the *Vancouver Sun*, the *News-Herald*, and, especially, the *Province*. By his own count, he produced more than six thousand columns on an unforgiving daily deadline. The columns were sparked by brief news items, chance encounters on the street, or whimsies of his imagination. His own failures at sport and a mortifying inability to navigate the treacherous waters of social situations gave his prose an everyman appeal. He was self-deprecating and never mean-spirited, except perhaps when describing his own physical attributes. In his telling, he carried a nose resembling a Roman aqueduct dividing small eyes "softened by their fine old leather pouches."

A sense of humour that earned a wide audience in the 1950s seemed dated as the decades passed. Despite his great loyalty to the *Province* (he worked without a contract and refused to holiday lest editors replace him), he was dismissed from its pages in 1986 without fanfare. Many believed he deserved better.

Nicol's career included a Broadway flop, an infamous literary hoax, and a conviction and fine for being in contempt of court.

In typical fashion, he described failure as "the sugar of life: the more lumps you take, the sweeter you are."

Eric Patrick Nicol was born in Kingston, Ontario, to Amelia Mannock and William Nicol. The family moved to Vancouver when he was young, then lived briefly in Nelson before returning to the coast.

Days after Nicol graduated from Lord Byng High School during the Depression, his father announced he had lost his job with a brokerage firm. He left to explore the possibility of opening a motor court in England. His mother took a part-time job as a clerk in a dress shop, while Eric earned tips as a golf caddy. His summer earnings, as well as a modest bursary, allowed him to enter classes at the University of British Columbia. One day, he slipped into the empty offices of the student newspaper to submit an anonymous contribution to a long-running satirical column called "Chang Suey," which lampooned campus figures through the misadventures of a fictional Chinese detective. In time, his identity was discovered. A senior editor of the *Ubyssey* offered the student a column of his own. It was to be called "The Mummery" and the bashful writer also received a

Biblical pseudonym in Jabez, Hebrew for "he who gives pain." The column and the byline were the brainstorm of a brash, confident Yukoner by the name of Pierre Berton. Nicol was delighted.

"If the two most satisfying sounds that a man can evoke from a woman are the moan of ecstasy and the hoot of laughter, I went for the giggle," Nicol wrote in *Anything for a Laugh*, a 1998 memoir. "For starters."

He continued with his studies, as well as composing regular contributions to the student newspaper, even as he realized his time in the campus officers training corps would soon force him into uniform on a more permanent basis.

"By 1941," he later wrote, "it was becoming plain that the war would not be over by Christmas in 1939, as I had been led to believe."

After graduating with honours in French, Nicol joined a ground crew of the Royal Canadian Air Force, which afforded him time to produce scripts for such radio variety shows as *Command Performance*. Back on campus, the Players' Club staged two of his comedies, *Her Scienceman Lover* and *Guthrie Meek in the Army, or, He's E2 in the Army but he's A1 in my Heart*.

Having escaped hostilities, he resumed studies at the Sorbonne after the war. A $10 fee for each column published back home afforded him a week's dining in Parisian restaurants. "Popular opinion to the contrary, it isn't always springtime in Paris," he wrote. "The other seasons are autumn, winter and tourist." A collection of his articles was published as *Twice Over Lightly* by the Ryerson Press in 1947. His long-time house was owned by the United Church, somewhat restricting his more ribald wordplay. "I couldn't get away with even a *single* entendre," he complained.

An offer to write variety sketches for the BBC led him to abandon his studies, as he prepared scripts for *Leave Your Name and Number* and, later, *Breakfast with Braden*, the latter produced by Pat Dixon, an eccentric who would later be responsible for producing the madcap *Goon Show*.

Back home in Vancouver, Nicol sometimes interrupted his

daily yuk for a more serious examination of the events of the day. In 1954, William Gash, nineteen, was convicted of murder and sentenced to death in the bludgeoning of forty-five-year-old Frank Pitsch, whose body was found on the thirteenth fairway of a local golf course. Both men made a meagre living by hunting lost golf balls.

After the conviction, Nicol wrote an allegory in which he confesses his guilt before God for his responsibility as an "unwilling accomplice" in the execution of young Gash. As a piece of writing, it was a scathing critique of capital punishment. Alas, Justice J.V. Clyne found the column to be "exaggerated and heavy-handed" and, more importantly, contemptuous of the Gash jurors, who were described by Nicol as being "the twelve persons who planned the murder." The judge fined the newspaper $2,500 and Nicol $250 for contempt.

As it turned out, the killer's sentence was commuted to life imprisonment six days before his scheduled execution.

More painful to Nicol was the attempt to bring to Broadway his stage play *Like Father, Like Fun*, which enjoyed success in Vancouver. The effort was plagued from the start, including a need to change the title to the less memorable *A Minor Adjustment*. Meanwhile, the acerbic comic Don Rickles, whom Nicol thought perfect for his play, withdrew from the production. The plot featured a lumber baron conniving to have one of his mistresses seduce his son so as to remove from the scene the chaste but unwelcome girl next door. It was not well received.

Clive Barnes of the *New York Times* called it a "non-play about non-people . . . as flat as Holland and as sparkling as mud . . . an opaque mediocrity, harmless and witless." The comedy opened at the Brooks Atkinson Theatre on October 6, 1967. It closed on October 7.

The lesson learned by the author: "I and Abraham Lincoln should have stayed out of the theatre."

The unhappy experience led Nicol to write a book titled *A Scar is Born*. He kept producing stage plays, including *The Fourth*

Monkey, about a playwright retreating to a bucolic island, and *Pillar of Sand*. "The reviews were mixed," he said of the latter, "bad and terrible." Another comedy, about the crusty British Columbia newspaper proprietor Ma Murray, opened in Kamloops with the aged and ailing subject in attendance. In the midst of the opening-night production, she demanded from the balcony, in a voice heard throughout the theatre, "Who are these people and what are they doing?" It brought down the house.

Always eager for mischief, Nicol was prodded by publisher Douglas Gibson to create a fictitious account of the true-life misadventures of Francis Dickens, the son of Charles, who served without distinction in the North-West Mounted Police. Presented as a series of frontier letters by the hapless policeman edited by Nicol, the novel succeeded in convincing several reviewers of their authenticity. (The hoax was aided by a respected university archivist posing with yellowed documents, ostensibly the letters, but in fact aged laundry lists from a steamship company.) The brilliant opening line should have given away the game to all but the most credulous: "It was not the best of times, it was not the worst of times, it was Ottawa."

Dickens of the Mounted was a runaway bestseller, appearing, according to the *Encyclopedia of Literature in Canada*, on both fiction and non-fiction lists.

After his long run at the *Province* ended, Nicol continued to produce books at a regular pace. In 1995, he became the inaugural winner of the George Woodcock Lifetime Achievement Award for an exemplary literary career in British Columbia. This was followed by his being invested into the Order of Canada, which recognized his use of humour to address serious issues such as racism and capital punishment.

He was asked once why he kept working.

"Writers never retire," he said, "they just die."

He did so in Vancouver, aged ninety-one.

May 23, 2011

A beloved figure in the Province *newsroom, Jeani Read, shown here in 1993, was a no-nonsense journalist, who went from covering rock 'n' roll to becoming a must-read columnist.* PHOTO BY ARLEN REDEKOP, PROVIDED BY THE *PROVINCE*

JEANI READ

JOURNALIST

(FEBRUARY 12, 1947—DECEMBER 21, 2007)

Rod Stewart greeted her at the door to his hotel room clad only in underwear and a sexy, pop-star pout. Rod the Mod had *amour* in mind, but Jeani Read arrived armed with pen and notepad in search of nothing more thrilling than *bons mots*.

Stylish in dress and energetic in style, Read herself could have been mistaken for a star. As a freelance critic, her eager approach and prolific coverage managed to create a rock music beat where none had existed in the pages of the *Province*, a morning broadsheet in Vancouver not previously known for being attuned to popular music. She was a rare woman in any city to be covering rock in those days, perhaps excusing Stewart's mistaken impression as to the reason for her appearance at his room.

In 1971, the *Georgia Straight* described her arriving at a cocktail party for Elton John in "buckskin hot pants and a matching midicoat." She immediately nabbed the star for a quick, exclusive interview.

Kind and gentle in person, she could be a ferocious interviewer. Tom Harrison, her successor as the paper's rock critic, describes an incident in which Billy Joel waited to be interviewed by Ms. Read backstage. "She came flying in, wearing a fur coat, boa scarf, floppy hat and carrying an oversized handbag that contained her interview notes," Harrison wrote. "Behind her large-framed glasses, she seemed flustered. Right, thought Joel, as he observed this apparently ditzy female, piece of cake. Jeani's first question to him, once her nervous energy had been relatively contained, was, 'Why do you hate women?'" Joel later pronounced it the most difficult interview of his career.

When she reviewed George Harrison's first North American solo tour after the breakup of the Beatles, her opinion was reprinted in a feature article by *Rolling Stone* magazine.

"All I could think about was Dylan a few months ago," she wrote in 1974, "singing all his songs wrong for all the people who wanted to hear them the way they were used to hearing them. Because Harrison sang most of his songs wrong, too. Except the painful difference was that Dylan was in complete control of what he was doing. It was an extraordinary experience in image breaking, of personal integrity. And George—well, George didn't seem as if he knew what he was doing at all."

Her enthusiasm waned in the late 1970s as she tired of rock's banality. Finding little in punk to rekindle her interest, she abandoned music to write a lifestyles column. It was called "Stayin' Alive," which, incidentally, was the title of a contemporary Bee Gees hit. She brought an unpredictability and a certain freewheeling sensibility owing much to her own coming of age in the 1960s. The column made her one of Vancouver's best-known journalists. In a city where newspaper columnists succeeded by writing about exotic nightlife or the even more bizarre world of BC politics, Read found a readership by exploring the topics of morality and behaviour that in an earlier age would have been dismissed as women's issues.

BC Bookworld magazine described her style as "cryptic and often witty." Her prose was idiosyncratic to be sure, yet it was eminently readable. She drove certain readers mad—usually men. Rafe Mair, the radio hotline host who had been a Social Credit cabinet minister, dismissed her in the *Financial Post* as a "columnist of the hard-left feminist persuasion."

A short newspaper blurb or overheard snippet of conversation could give birth to a column. "She just kept her ear to the ground," said her husband, Michael Mercer, a playwright and writer for television. "It was very much as things came."

A 1992 column about the Ontario court battle over women's right to walk topless in public made several piquant observations. Read agreed with the women's position, yet teased them for not campaigning for, say, universal breast screening. She also offered her support to topless dancers—"exploited by the patriarchy on one hand and treated with contempt by their sisters on the other." She finished the column by noting she would be attending the upcoming Vancouver Folk Festival ("a pioneer breast-rights venue"), but not an upcoming protest march in Ontario, preferring instead to "wait for the next inalienable-rights demonstration, when men across the country participate in a Winkie Walk."

A collection of her more provocative columns, titled *Endless Summers and Other Shared Hallucinations*, was published by Flight Press in 1985.

Jeananne Patricia Read was born in Shanghai in 1947 to George Read, a British accountant, and the former Elfreida Ennock, an exotic beauty of German-Estonian ancestry. Ennock was born in 1920 in Vladivostok, the Siberian city that became an outpost of opposition to Bolshevik revolutionists. Her family was forced to flee to Shanghai. She met her husband among the expatriates living in the Chinese city's International Settlement. They married in 1940, spending four years in Japanese internment. After the family immigrated to Canada, Elfreida Read spent time in a sanatorium for treatment of tuberculosis. At this time, a female relative helped care for Jeani, who spoke some Russian as a child. Her mother recovered to enjoy a career as a poet, memoirist and children's author.

Jeani graduated from the University of British Columbia with an English degree. Her career at the *Province* spanned a transition from broadsheet to tabloid, as well as countless editorial regime changes. The *Georgia Straight* saw the loss of her column some years ago as a reflection of the newspaper's taking a more monotonous political tone, as liberal voices disappeared and those of a conservative bent became ascendant.

In the months before her death, Read's considerable talents were called on to explore the intricacies of home renovations. She also handled such lifestyles features as "Girl Talk" and "Bachelor of the Week." If the assignments seemed somewhat lesser than the person assigned to them, Read remained as diligent as ever in crafting readable vignettes.

It must also be said she was a welcome presence in the newsroom, where female colleagues enjoyed her friendship and male colleagues quietly nursed their crushes. She was known for her teasing office debates with Jim Taylor, a sports columnist who held an antipathy to feminism and baseball, both of which she ably defended.

She once dated Bruce Allen, the crusty rock promoter whose first great success was Bachman-Turner Overdrive. They had met at school in 1963, where Allen remembers a brilliant, award-winning student. It was Read who suggested to her boyfriend that he name his fledgling booking agency and management company after himself, and it is still known as Bruce Allen Talent.

The couple befriended Jack Wasserman, the *Vancouver Sun*'s legendary chronicler of saloon life, for whom Read did research. The columnist provided entree to the city's thriving club scene, as well as to the raucous newspaper business.

Read met future husband Michael Mercer at a reception held for poet Leonard Cohen. She wrote scripts with her husband, one of which, an episode of *The Beachcombers* titled "Computer Error," was nominated for a 1988 Gemini Award.

The couple also collaborated on a letter to the editor of the *Globe and Mail*, suggesting the phenomenon known as the "brain drain" instead become known as the "greed bleed."

In 1999, her husband suffered kidney failure. In searching for a donor, it was discovered that she was a match. She immediately volunteered to donate her kidney, which Mercer still carries.

The failure of her health came with stunning speed. Cancer of the esophagus was diagnosed only a few weeks before her death. Her passing was so unexpected that another newspaper in the CanWest newspaper chain reprinted one of her articles postmortem without noting her passing.

Her untimely death meant she did not get to work on a project she had long contemplated—a Canadian version of William Least Heat-Moon's *Blue Highways*, a nostalgic travelogue of rural roads.

January 24, 2008

LEILA VENNEWITZ

HEINRICH BÖLL'S TRANSLATOR

(NOVEMBER 29, 1912—AUGUST 8, 2007)

Leila Vennewitz was one of the great postwar translators of German literature, bringing the works of Heinrich Böll and others to an English-language audience.

Critics raved about her efforts. Reviewers in the *New York Times* praised her for "lucidly," "impeccably" and "unobtrusively" translating original German texts. The *Montreal Gazette* called her incomparable.

She would be Böll's sole English translator for nearly a quarter-century, while he enjoyed his most widespread critical and popular success.

Vennewitz won several major awards, although few in her adopted land knew who she was. She "lived quietly and largely unheralded in Vancouver for more than fifty years," noted *BC BookWorld*.

Born Leila Croot at Portsmouth, Hampshire, England, she showed a precocious talent in languages while attending Moira House Girls School in East Sussex. After graduation, she spent a year at the Sorbonne in Paris, where, at age eighteen, she took up German, which she spoke at first with a French accent.

She joined her older brother in Hong Kong in 1934. She married the journalist Hans Melchers, a union that produced a daughter before ending in divorce. She remarried, rarely ever again speaking of her first husband. Her second husband, William Vennewitz, was born in China to a long-established merchant family of German ancestry. The couple lived in Shanghai, protected during the Japanese occupation by his connections to an Axis country.

William Vennewitz opposed the Nazis, sending his daughter to German-language school with permission not to deliver the stiff-armed "Heil, Hitler" salute. After the defeat of the Japanese, he was declared an enemy alien, despite his politics, and deported to Germany, where he spent a year in an internment camp.

In 1947, Leila Vennewitz went back to her homeland on vacation with her daughter. She never returned to China. Communist forces occupied Shanghai, and she and her husband decided to build their lives anew. They immigrated to Canada in 1949, opening an import-export business for pharmaceutical chemicals. She found work as a legal secretary.

A friend from Shanghai days asked her to translate his book about the uneasy partnership between the Soviet Union and Communist China. Klaus Mehnert's *Peking and Moscow* (1963) became an international bestseller and her new career was launched.

She began handling Böll's works in 1965, when she translated *The Clown*. Four years later, she won the prestigious Schlegel-Tieck Prize for German translation from the Society of Authors of London for her handling of *End of a Mission*. She would be Böll's lone English translator until 1988, handling novels, essays and short stories, as well as articles for such publications as *Esquire*, *Harper's* and *The New Yorker*.

The German author was awarded the Nobel Prize in Literature in 1972, an honour owed in part to widespread popularity made possible by the skill of his English translator. The Nobel Foundation credits Vennewitz with translations of nineteen Böll publications. Her work on his *And Never Said a Word* took the Goethe House PEN Prize in 1979, and a decade later, she was named the recipient of an American Translator's Association prize for Martin Walser's *Breakers*.

In 1997, she won the Helen and Kurt Wolff Prize for her translation of Jurek Becker's novel *Jacob the Liar*. Other authors whose works she translated into English include Uwe Timm, Uwe Johnson, Hermann Hesse, Alexander Kluge, Friedrich Durrenmatt and Walter Kempowski.

Vennewitz championed the cause of translators receiving full credit for their work, once chastising a *Globe and Mail* reviewer for praising the literary quality of a book originally written in Italian without noting it had been translated.

Another *Globe* review led her to write a letter to the editor correcting three errors—the nationality of the author of *Wilhelm Tell* (German, not Swiss); the German spelling of Lake Lucerne (Vierwaldstattersee); and the interpretation of the French word *rivage* ("shore" rather than "view").

In recent years, she donated her papers and manuscripts to the Lilly Library at Indiana University, which holds a modest collection of Böll's correspondence with his American literary agent. She also created a fund in her name at the library, providing financial support to translators.

A rare criticism of her work was levelled by authors of a 1986 literary study, "Call of Human Nature: The Role of Scatology in Modern German Literature." While acknowledging her brilliance as a translator, Dieter and Jacqueline Rollfinke disagreed with her interpretation of *Mistbande* ("bunch of manure") as "rabble."

September 29, 2007

ATHLETES

The feisty boxer Jimmy McLarnin strikes his trademark pose in the late 1920s. During a thirteen-year professional career, McLarnin twice won the world welterweight championship. He was a rare fighter to leave the racket with both his money and his marbles. PHOTO PROVIDED BY THE BC SPORTS HALL OF FAME & MUSEUM

Jimmy (Baby Face) McLarnin

WORLD WELTERWEIGHT BOXING CHAMPION

(DECEMBER 19, 1907—OCTOBER 28, 2004)

Jimmy McLarnin, a slip of a boy, endured beatings while defending his newsboy turf at the Vancouver dockyards, a prized spot to sell the *Daily Province*. He learned to take a punch at the waterfront. After his father bought a pair of boxing gloves, he learned how to throw one.

Young Jimmy soon fell under the tutelage of a stevedore whose harsh experiences in the ring and on the battlefield failed to extinguish a generosity rare among his kind in the boxing fraternity. Charles (Pop) Foster was a trainer and manager who offered tactical advice in the ring and strategic wisdom in selecting fighters outside it.

Foster saw in the skinny kid the possibilities of a world-class fighter, a proposal so unlikely as to be laughable. Yet he proved to be right: McLarnin went on to twice hold the world welterweight title.

Handsome as a choirboy, McLarnin was called "Baby Face." For years, tough men tried to rearrange his features while attempting to knock his block off. Some defeated him, and one even knocked him out, yet he marked his eighty-fifth birthday with nary a scar on his face.

In his day, McLarnin's name was as famous as those friends with whom he hobnobbed from Broadway to Hollywood. He taught Babe Ruth to box over drinks at Dinty Moore's chophouse and ate a slice of lemon pie with the gangster Legs Diamond. The boxer starred in newsreels and magazines, golfed with Bob Hope and Bing Crosby, squired Jean Harlow and Barbara Stanwyck. Away from the cameras, he politely turned down Mae West's entreaty to come up and see her some time; he was carrying a torch for a girl back home.

Newspapermen loved him, for he fit every Irish stereotype except that of the drunkard. Reporters who sometimes scripted an athlete's clever comments had no need to do so with McLarnin, whose wit befit the primitive appeal of his sport.

"The only time he touched me," he once said of an opponent, "was when we shook hands in the ring at the start of the fight."

Unlike many in his racket, McLarnin left the fight game with his money and his wits.

James McLarnin was born in 1907 in Magherageery, outside Belfast, in what is now Northern Ireland, the fifth child of what would be an even dozen. The young family immigrated to Canada three years later, settling on a wheat farm near Mortlach, Saskatchewan. The wet miseries of an Irish winter were paradise compared to the Prairie cold, so the McLarnins moved to Vancouver where they lived in a modest house at 662 Union Street in the rough-and-tumble Strathcona neighbourhood.

Samuel McLarnin, a butcher by trade, opened a second-hand furniture store, while his son contributed to the family's keep by hawking newspapers. One day, the father was watching the son kick a soccer ball when he was approached by Pop Foster, a longshoreman with a bum leg. As recounted in 1950 by Ralph Allen in a memorable profile for *Maclean's*, Foster admired Jimmy's running. He said to Sam McLarnin: "I could make a boxer of that boy."

"What kind of a boxer?" the father asked.

"The only kind that's worth making. A champion."

"A champion of what?"

"A champion of the world."

One of the odder boxing partnerships was born in that moment.

Few would be as successful. None would be as lasting. A veteran wounded three times in the Boer War and once during the Great War, Foster had spent his youth as a booth fighter on the carnival circuit in Britain. His act was to fight all comers—any man, any weight. A challenger earned a pound for every round they lasted, an attractive prize in the Victorian era. A pound-a-round fighter like Foster only survived by dispatching opponents quickly, otherwise he might end a long day poor, hungry and beaten.

Young Jimmy McLarnin possessed a crushing right, honed on the chins of other newsboys. Foster, a gruff Yorkshireman, knew a one-punch fighter had limited prospects, so during training sessions he tethered his pupil's stronger hand behind his back. Tutorials in southpaw fisticuffs were followed by lessons in footwork. Sawdust was sprinkled across the floor of the basement of his father's store so the young fighter could learn to glide like a dancer.

In time, a crunching right hand would be McLarnin's greeting card in the ring, a corkscrew left hook his way of bidding adieu.

He established himself as a comer by winning two of three bouts against Fidel LaBarba, a Los Angeles high-school student recently returned from the Olympic Games in Paris with the gold medal in the flyweight division. Their third fight was a draw.

In 1926, his fortunes soured when he lost three of five fights. Declared washed up at nineteen, the boxer abandoned the West Coast for Chicago, where he faced the fierce Louis (Kid) Kaplan. The first punch broke McLarnin's jaw. After submitting to three rounds of beating, he returned to his corner where Pop Foster had some advice. "Jimmy," he said, "why don't *you* try hitting *him*?" Kaplan was floored in the eighth round. The win earned McLarnin his first shot at a title. He faced slick Sammy Mandell at the Polo Grounds in New York, but the champion proved elusive, thwarting the challenger with deft left jabs. The fifteen-round fight ended with a unanimous decision, the verdict visible on McLarnin's face, as his left eye was swollen shut and blood streamed from his nose. He was, read one account, "a sorry sight." Five years passed before he got another shot.

In New York, McLarnin became the hero of one of the city's ethnic clans and the nemesis of another. Reporters called McLarnin the "Irish Lullaby," the "Baby-Faced Assassin," the "Beltin' Celt" and the "Murderous Mick." The sportswriter Paul Gallico called him "hell's own cherub."

In boxing's unsubtle marketing, fortunes were to be made pitting an Irish Republican (even if he had been raised a Methodist) against sons of the synagogue. So McLarnin fought a procession of Jewish boxers, knocking out Sid (Ghost of the Ghetto) Terris in one round, Ruby (Jewel of the Ghetto) Goldstein in two, Al (Battling Bronco of the Bronx) Singer in three, and the great Benny Leonard in six. Those fights earned McLarnin nicknames he always hated: Hebrew Scourge and Jew Beater. "The Irish wanted to see me beat the Jews and the Jewish fans wanted to see me beaten," he once told me. "That's how it was."

A chance for redemption from his earlier title defeat came in Los Angeles on May 29, 1933, when he faced welterweight champ Young Corbett III, an Italian southpaw born Raffaele Giordano. McLarnin needed just two minutes, thirty-seven seconds for a knockout. "It all happened so fast I didn't have time to pray," said Sam McLarnin, who was at ringside to see his son fight for the first time. After fourteen tough years, Pop Foster's ridiculous promise had come true—Jimmy McLarnin was world champion. In Vancouver, the manager of a movie house halted a screening to announce the news; the newspaper young Jimmy had hawked ran banner headlines; trolley-car drivers rang their bells.

His next three fights, all with the title in the balance, occurred against Barney Ross. These were vicious affairs between two ferocious fighters. They began the showdown as rivals, and ended it as legends. McLarnin lost the title in a split decision on May 28, 1934, won it back again on another split decision on September 17, then lost it for good in a unanimous decision on May 28, 1935.

Their ultimate battle, before forty thousand fans at baseball's Polo Grounds, under the eye of referee Jack Dempsey, turned into a brutal slugfest by the eighth round. Ross, his left hand broken, absorbed a series of left hooks to the head before retaliating with an onslaught of rights. Exhausted, the pair abandoned all pretense of artistry to simply unload whatever punches they had left. The decision earned a cascade of boos. Spectators debated the merit of the verdict, but none doubted they had witnessed boxing history.

McLarnin fought only three more times, ending his career with a decisive pounding of Lou Ambers on November 20, 1936. He retired with a record of sixty-three wins, eleven losses and three draws. Only once did he not finish a fight on his feet.

McLarnin did well in life's neutral corner. After a long courtship, he married Lillian Cupit, a Vancouver teacher. After winning an estimated $500,000 US, he was able to resist the lure of hefty purses for a comeback. He golfed, dabbled with investments and attended the Cauliflower Alley Club in Los Angeles with other retired boxers and wrestlers.

"I never met a fighter I didn't like," McLarnin said. "Thing is, they were always trying to knock my ears off."

When Pop Foster died in 1956, McLarnin and his wife received two-thirds of an estate estimated at $200,000 US in cash and bonds. Most of the remainder went to the four McLarnin children.

Following the death of his wife in 1985, McLarnin moved to eastern Washington state, where three of his four children live. Decades after he had hung up his gloves, he was only three pounds over his fighting weight. He invited a guest to squeeze his bicep, struck an ancient pugilistic pose, and pantomimed the telling blows from his championship bouts by dancing across his kitchen floor. He eventually receded into a dementia that made it difficult for him to speak. He accompanied his daughter on day trips and always enjoyed a slice of his favourite pie on his birthday, yet ate only the pecan filling. Whatever the fog of his memory, he remembered a fighter does not eat fatty pie crust.

He was buried at Forest Lawn Memorial Park in Glendale, California, between the graves of his wife and his manager.

November 29, 2004

The World's Strongest Man didn't have trouble attracting the ladies and, as can be seen in this 1954 photo, he didn't have trouble hoisting them, either. ARTRAY PHOTO, PROVIDED BY THE VANCOUVER PUBLIC LIBRARY, 82602J

Doug Hepburn

WORLD'S STRONGEST MAN
(SEPTEMBER 16, 1926—NOVEMBER 22, 2000)

Doug Hepburn was born cross-eyed and with a club foot. The scrawny boy took up weightlifting as a defence against the cruelties of schoolyard bullies. In time, he claimed the title World's Strongest Man.

After becoming a world champion weightlifter in 1953, he was cheered by the very citizens who had once sneered at his aspirations. Hepburn never forgave them for the earlier snub and spent much of his life nursing a grudge, a big man with big beefs.

Hepburn spent his final years living as a recluse. He had a circle of friends, but often found solace in solitude. He was a nearly forgotten figure by the time he died in Vancouver of a perforated ulcer.

He eked out a living of sorts by peddling health foods and exercise equipment. A website offered photographs for sale at $10 each, as well as fifty coin-operated arm-wrestling machines ("Make me an offer!"). He was a poet, inventor, dietitian, cabaret singer and storefront philosopher.

"In India," he once said, "a great athlete is seen as being very close to God. He's worshipped in some places."

Hepburn was once venerated for Herculean feats of lifting, but he was as uncomfortable with praise as he certainly was with ridicule. He heard plenty of both.

Douglas Ivan Hepburn was the product of a union so shortlived that it was over before he could walk. As a baby, he was sent to live with his grandfather in Edmonton. He was later reunited with his mother in his Vancouver birthplace.

He was beaten often by bullies at school. An operation to repair his deformed foot ended in failure in his teens. His ankle lost its flexibility and his right leg was forever after shorter than his left. Surgery corrected his eyes, but it did nothing for whatever unspoken hurt he nursed inside.

After quitting school midway through Grade 11, Hepburn was kicked out of the family home by his stepfather. He worked as a lifeguard by day and a bouncer by night. (The lifeguards were having problems with a local gang until the day Hepburn hoisted a 120-kilogram rowboat overhead. The gang went elsewhere.)

Working without a coach, finding instruction from glossy magazines bought at the local drugstore, Hepburn determined to become a world-class weightlifter. His dream was mocked in his hometown.

After beating John Davis for the US weightlifting championship in 1952, Hepburn inexplicably was left off the Canadian Olympic team. Davis went on to win the gold medal at Helsinki.

Hepburn performed lifting exhibitions during baseball games in Seattle to raise money to attend the world championships in Sweden. He won, claiming the title of World's Strongest Man. He was so broke that he spent his first night as world champion back home in Vancouver at a $3-a-night hotel.

The mayor hired Hepburn as a $150-a-month bodyguard, thus preserving his amateur status and guaranteeing that Hepburn was around when Vancouver played host to the British Empire and Commonwealth Games in the summer of 1954.

Hepburn won the gold medal with a 370-pound press, a 300-pound snatch and a 370-pound jerk.

Lord Alexander of Tunis, a war hero and former governor-general of Canada, presented the medal with the exclamation: "You're quite a man."

Hepburn replied: "You're quite a fella yourself."

He expected the city would reward his great feat, but things did not turn out as he had hoped. Until the day he died, Hepburn believed the city reneged on a promise to build him a gymnasium.

He complained bitterly for decades and long entertained the idea of opening a gym for abused and neglected street kids.

One night, the 275-pound Mr. Hepburn was presented to wrestling promoter Joe Malcewicz, the handler of such eye-poking, hair-pulling terrors as Yukon Eric and Gorgeous George.

"Of course, Malcewicz had seen them all," Hepburn later recounted. "He says, 'Take your shirt off.' Well, I do, and his eyes bug out like celery sticks. There were dollar signs in those eyes. He saw a million dollars on the hoof right there in front of him.

"But I was just a poor, dumb weightlifter. I was so naive and ignorant I didn't know why he was staring. My eyes would bug out if you put a thousand dollars in my hand. I didn't know you could make that wrestling in one night."

Wrestling wasn't for the gentle giant, as it turned out, and Hepburn handled a few engagements as a lounge singer. Soon, he was wrestling with the bottle and checked into one institution where the drying-out cure included experimenting with the hallucinogen LSD.

He continued to lift weights long after his retirement from competition, issuing challenges to others of his age.

"All the trouble I got into was the result of me refusing to conform," he said. "A man who doesn't conform usually gets himself in trouble. Conforming means being normal. But then how do you do the extraordinary?"

December 13, 2000

Bill Werbeniuk lines up a shot at the Big Game pool hall in Port Moody in 1992. Big Bill was a remarkable figure in a colourful sport not lacking for characters. PHOTO BY ARLEN REDEKOP, PROVIDED BY THE *PROVINCE*

BILL WERBENIUK

SNOOKER PLAYER

(JANUARY 14, 1947—JANUARY 20, 2003)

The championship snooker player Big Bill Werbeniuk drank lots of lager before, during and after a match to steady what he—and his doctors, he was quick to add—described as a hereditary nervous tremor in his cue arm.

The Winnipeg native was a Falstaffian character readily recognizable for his girth. He became a cult figure in Britain during snooker's heyday, when players dressed in tuxedos and white-gloved referees patrolled the green baize table. It was during a televised 1980 World Cup match against England that Werbeniuk leaned far over the table for an awkward shot only to have his pants split in the seat. The audience's merriment was fuelled by Werbeniuk's decision that day not to wear underpants.

Tales of his alcohol consumption made him a legend. It was said he drank thirty, forty or fifty pints every match. Werbeniuk once admitted to downing seventy-six cans of lager while relieving a tournament's victors of their prize money in an after-hours challenge.

Fans applauded his ability to hold liquor while playing world-class snooker. He even convinced the taxman that his beer consumption was necessary in the exercise of his livelihood and thus was a deductible expense. That victory, perhaps his most famous, proved only temporary and he was later ordered to pay up.

Hired to spend an evening at a pub in Middlesbrough, Werbeniuk was surprised not to be asked to perform trick shots, or to play against local amateurs, as was the custom for a hired professional. So great was his popularity that he was paid £500 simply to sit on a barstool. "No snooker, just to knock back a few pints all night," Werbeniuk recalled, marvelling at his good fortune.

The prodigious beer drinking placed stress on his heart, for which he took Inderal, a beta blocker. When it was listed as a banned substance by snooker's governing body, Werbeniuk refused to change his medical regimen. He was fined and suspended before abandoning England and his professional career. He spent the final decade of his life in anonymity, sharing a Vancouver apartment with his mother and brother.

Tales of his drinking unfairly overshadowed his considerable snooker skills. Werbeniuk was a terrific long-ball potter with formidable cue power. He was capable of recording sizable breaks, notably a record-tying clearance of 142 points at the world championship in 1979. Werbeniuk also was clever in his tactical strategy.

Still, he seemed never to achieve his full promise as a player. He was ranked as high as No. 8 in the world, yet failed to win a major tournament outside Canada. His best performance at the world championships was in reaching the quarter-finals four times. He had greater success teaming with compatriots Kirk Stevens and Cliff Thorburn, with whom he won the World Cup in 1982.

William Alexander Werbeniuk was born to snooker. His grandfather, a Ukrainian immigrant, owned Pop's Billiards on Logan Avenue in Winnipeg's tough downtown core. Bill's father was known as Shorty, a formidable player with a neighbourhood reputation more as a felon than a father. At age twelve, Bill took one unsuspecting adult player for $600.

Werbeniuk moved to Vancouver in 1967, hooking up with Thorburn at Pender Billiards. The pair hired an ex-heavyweight fighter to accompany them as they toured pool halls in search of shooters with more greenbacks than good sense. Werbeniuk was called "The Garbage Collector"; his job in the hustle was to act the untalented shooter against whom the locals, having just been fleeced by Thorburn, thought they would win back their money.

Werbeniuk and Thorburn would be friends and rivals for the next fifteen years, competing for Canadian and North American championships before seeking their fortunes in England.

The nature of their friendship was on display at the Professional Players Tournament at Sutton Coldfield in 1982. When the referee penalized Thorburn a frame for arriving ten minutes late, Werbeniuk announced he would deliberately lose the next frame. The penalty was revoked and Werbeniuk enjoyed an untainted 5–2 victory. That same year, Werbeniuk halted play at his table during the World Cup to watch Thorburn complete a break of 147 at an adjacent table. It was the first perfect clearance to be televised and Werbeniuk celebrated by giving Thorburn a bear hug.

Although he had been playing for money since elementary school, Werbeniuk officially turned professional in 1973. Billed as "Burly, Battling Bill Werbeniuk," he beat Atomic Eddie Agha of Montreal and his friend Thorburn to claim the Canadian title. Werbeniuk also won the North American pro title that year, overcoming Thorburn and succeeding him as champion. He would retain the title for the following three years, at which time the competition was suspended.

Werbeniuk spent about nine months each year plying his trade in Britain. He lived in a converted bus and hung out at the North Midland Snooker Centre at Worksop.

He reached the quarter-finals of the Embassy World Championship at the Crucible Theatre in Sheffield in 1978 (losing 13–6 to Ray Reardon), 1979 (losing 13–9 to John Virgo), 1981 (losing 13–10 to Reardon) and 1983 (losing 13–11 to Alex Higgins). He had a record-tying break of 142 at the Crucible in 1979 and, after a perfect 147 was recorded by Thorburn in 1983, compiled a high break of 143 in the 1985 tournament.

His frustration at the Crucible was matched in several prominent tournaments, as victory proved elusive. He was defeated in the semifinal of the United Kingdom Championship in 1979; lost 7–3 to Thorburn at the finals of the Winfield Masters in Australia in 1983; and lost 9–5 to Steve Davis, then at the peak of his considerable talent, at the 1983 Lada Classic in Warrington, England.

Even success at the 1982 World Cup was bookended by a loss in the 1980 final to Wales and in the 1986 final to Ireland.

Over the years, the beer drinking proved less able to ease the effects of Werbeniuk's condition, which was diagnosed as familial benign essential tremor. His game went into a decline.

He also found himself embroiled in a dispute with the World Professional Billiards and Snooker Association. The governing body adopted a list of banned drugs after some players had been caught indulging. Among the banned drugs was Inderal.

Werbeniuk chose exile after he was fined and suspended, making a final appearance in England at a qualifying match for the Crucibles. He lost 10–1 to Nigel Bond, saying afterwards, "I drank twenty-eight pints of lager and eight double scotches during the day and was only starting to feel comfortable at the table in the final couple of frames. Now I know that I can only play if I'm totally drunk, and that's not fair on me."

He returned to Canada for good, earning spending money by teaching pool, a game he did not particularly enjoy. One enterprising British reporter visited Werbeniuk at his local pub, The Jolly Coachman, in suburban Pitt Meadows, noting with admiration how Werbeniuk ordered round after round with "an imperceptible nod, a bit like someone bidding at Sotheby's."

The reporter also said he had learned the secret of Werbeniuk's ability to consume enormous amounts of alcohol—undiagnosed hypoglycemia.

Werbeniuk, who lived on a disability pension, spent the last three months of his life in hospital. He died of heart failure at age fifty-six. He was single and had no children. A brief marriage at age nineteen was unconsummated; the act was a favour for a woman seeking a residency permit.

January 29, 2003

FRANK WILLIAMS

BASEBALL PITCHER

(FEBRUARY 13, 1958—JANUARY 9, 2009)

Frank Williams, given up for adoption at birth, overcame his un-promising beginning to become a major-league pitcher. Hard work took him to the apex of his sport, but good fortune soured after he suffered injuries in a car wreck. His fall from baseball grace was sudden, his personal decline a much longer affair. He spent his final days on the streets of Victoria, where he was known as an alcoholic.

A popular figure blessed with a winning personality, Williams told a story as well as he threw a pitch.

His later years could be dismissed for having been lost to sub-stance abuse. Yet the years he spent on Vancouver Island at the end of his playing career were ones in which he explored his aboriginal roots, forging extended family connections among the Nuu-chah-nulth nations along the West Coast.

A humble demeanour and modesty about his own talent did not earn Williams a prominent profile as a major-league pitcher. In 333 games, he had but one assignment as a starter, during which he threw a complete-game shut out. The San Francisco Giants, Cincinnati Reds and Detroit Tigers all used the right-hander as a middle reliever. The role lacks glamour, but insiders recognize the

Frank Williams, who was given up for adoption at birth, overcame long odds to become a major-league pitcher for six seasons. He pitched for the Cincinnati Reds, as shown in this 1987 card. Williams wound up living on the streets in Victoria.
PHOTO COURTESY OF COMC.COM

importance of maintaining a lead, or preventing the opposition from turning a narrow advantage into a rout. Williams performed his job with quiet competence.

He came into the world accompanied by a twin brother with whom he would forge a bond beyond that with any other person. Born to a tubercular mother, who already had seven children at home, the boys were left behind to be named by the staff at a Seattle hospital. One was called Frank, the other Francis.

They would not know the story of their origins for many years to come. Their first four years were spent in a series of foster homes, including one in which they were so underfed Frank Williams would later remember stealing dry dog food from a cupboard.

The twins were rescued from a Dickensian fate by being taken into the comfortable middle-class home of a Boeing aircraft engineer. Dick McCullough, born with a withered right arm, believed in sport as an outlet for children. One spring morning, the Williams boys awoke to receive an Easter basket containing a baseball and a glove.

They grew up in Kirkland, Washington, a Seattle suburb that billed itself as "Baseball Town USA." Frank became a star pitcher, Francis his catcher on sandlot diamonds. The boys found an identity on the diamond, though they struggled as teenagers to understand their own place in the world. They were foster children carrying the family name of a biological father they had never met. With copper skin and moon faces, they knew they looked unlike their teammates. "We didn't even know we were Native," Frank Williams told me in 2001. "We had wavy hair and afros. We knew we weren't white."

As a teenager, Frank Williams was picked to join a combined team representing Kirkland in the senior Babe Ruth League tournament. The team won city, state and regional titles before winning a national championship at Sicks' Stadium in Seattle in August 1975.

As the twins prepared to set out on their own, they made a solemn pact. "We shook hands," Williams said. "Whoever makes it looks after the other."

He attended Shoreline Community College in Seattle before being lured to Lewis-Clark State College in Idaho, where coach Ed Cheff ran a stellar baseball program. In helping his recruit apply for financial aid, the coach learned the family background was as elusive as a knuckleball. Eventually, relatives were found at a Seattle housing project. It was then the boys learned of their aboriginal heritage, discovering as well an extended family with roots extending to Vancouver Island.

In one season with the Warriors, Williams lost more games than he won. He walked more batters than he struck out, but his earned-run average remained low because college opponents could not get around on a fastball usually timed at about nintety miles per hour.

At six foot one and 190 pounds, he had the size and the speed to attract the attention of scouts despite his disconcerting wildness around the plate. The Giants chose him in the eleventh round, No. 278 overall, of the 1979 free-agent draft.

In the minors, he pitched at Great Falls, Montana; Fresno, California; Shreveport, Louisiana; and Phoenix, Arizona. He struggled with control, leading the Pioneer League in hit batsmen in 1979, the California League in hit batsmen in 1981, and the Texas League in hit batsmen in 1982. While these beanings did not win him any friends among opponents, it showed a tough-nosed willingness to pitch inside. He began to strike out enough batters to earn a call-up to the big-league club.

While his fastball was good but not domineering, he became a much more effective hurler with mastery of a pitch in which the ball was held deep in the palm of his right hand. The ball was thrown as a curve, but acted on the way to the plate as a slider. The Williams' "slurve," as it was called, fooled many a batter left swinging at empty air.

In his third season, Williams enjoyed a 3–1 record with a miserly 1.20 earned-run average. Hardly anyone noticed. "He had as quiet a great year as any pitcher alive," noted *Bill Mazeroski's Baseball*, a respected annual.

The Giants traded him to the Reds for outfielder Eddie Milner in the off-season. Williams joined lefties Rob Murphy and John Franco as part of a superb bullpen staff. (Fifteen months after the trade, Milner would be suspended for cocaine use. This would later give rise to the contention the clubs had swapped troubled players.) By this time, Williams was earning nearly $500,000 per season and had married. Despite the newfound riches, he had a wild side. His college coach remembers watching in disbelief as the pitcher risked his livelihood by taking part in Tough Guy boxing competitions during the long Idaho winter.

Things were not well in Cincinnati, as the gambling of manager Pete Rose had come under scrutiny. Williams would later tell reporters about unsavory characters hanging around the manager's office.

He was let go after the 1988 season and appeared in forty-two games with the Tigers in 1989 before being released.

He then broke a bone in his neck and needed plastic surgery to repair his face after smashing into the windshield in a car wreck.

When his marriage collapsed, Williams moved to Vancouver Island, where he connected with his father's family at the Tseshaht First Nation at Port Alberni.

In 1992, a comeback attempt with an amateur team in Victoria fell far short. He worked in construction and did some house painting. His brother, who had suffered spinal nerve damage from a bicycle spill, joined him in the British Columbia capital. The injury made walking difficult for Francis. The brothers lamented they could no longer play catch.

In 2000, the Victoria fire department received an early morning call about a drug overdose at a notorious flophouse. Frank Williams was discovered unconscious on a filthy hallway floor. He stopped breathing, but was revived. One of the firefighters, Mark Perkins, recognized Williams. As it turned out, Perkins had pitched for the same Idaho college several years prior to Williams' arrival.

A few days later, Perkins returned to the flophouse with Walt Burrows, the Canadian supervisor for Major League Baseball's

Scouting Bureau. Burrows slipped a business card under the door, while Perkins left one of Williams' baseball cards as a signal they knew about his career. The former pitcher was put in touch with the Baseball Assistance Team, a charitable group that aids ballplayers who have fallen on hard times. Williams explained the overdose by insisting he had mistakenly snorted heroin instead of the cocaine he had asked for.

In 2004, Francis was killed when his basement apartment caught fire. The death troubled Frank Williams, who blamed himself for not being with his brother. In time, he became more of a street person, scavenging metal and kicking around downtown drop-in centres for the homeless. He earned pocket money by signing baseball cards at a downtown shop.

Ill from pneumonia, Williams went into a coma after suffering a heart attack. He died at Royal Jubilee Hospital in Victoria without regaining consciousness. Abandoned at birth, in death his bed was surrounded by family.

January 26, 2009

MEAN GENE KINISKI

WRESTLER

(NOVEMBER 23, 1928—APRIL 14, 2010)

Gene Kiniski was a mean, nasty, vicious scoundrel.

Fans threw shoes and chairs at him. One stabbed him in the back with a shiv.

More than once, a Kiniski match began in the ring only to be settled in the parking lot. He once drove an opponent's head into a parked car, leaving a large dent. Bent chrome featured prominently in a photograph in the next morning's newspaper.

His favourite move was known as the back-breaker. For nearly four decades, he was hated in three lands as the worst villain in professional wrestling. In 1960, the Toronto Shoe Repairmen named him "Heel of the Year." Everyone called him "Mean Gene."

Gosh, but he was a swell fellow.

A crew-cut behemoth with cauliflower ears, a baked-potato nose, and fingers as thick as kielbasa, Kiniski brought to his sport a wit as sharp as a hidden razor. He knew how to ballyhoo. He was under no illusions about the wrestling racket.

"Say you saw me in a fight on the street," he told the reporter John Mackie. "Regardless of whether you knew me or not, you'd say, 'Look at that big ugly son of a bitch kicking the [bleep] out of that guy.' I could care less what they said, as long as they paid to see me."

He called himself "Canada's greatest athlete" and who would argue against a wrestler capable of terrible deeds of destruction? Mean Gene is shown here committing mayhem within the ring during a 1976 bout. PHOTO BY BRIAN KENT, PROVIDED BY THE *VANCOUVER SUN*

Kiniski succumbed to cancer, his own body defeating him as no rival ever could.

He was an unforgettable character on television, standing six foot four, weighing 275 pounds, his speaking voice a rasp that sounded as if he gargled with crushed glass. Even his name was tough, those Polish consonants grinding against the vowels.

One of his shticks was to take over an interview with his own aggressive patter, cutting up his challengers with sharp words, teasing the fans who loved to hate him with promises of future mayhem, before handing the mic back with kind words about the skills of the interviewer.

Kiniski claimed the championships of the two major pro wrestling circuits, becoming one of the most familiar, if infamous, sporting figures of the 1960s.

The sportswriters called him "Big Thunder." He took as his own the title of "Canada's Greatest Athlete," the conceit being that any challenger first had to wrestle against him before competing in their own sport.

Who could beat Kiniski? The baseball pitcher Ferguson Jenkins? The golfer George Knudson? The jockey Sandy Hawley? Don't make me laugh. Only football's Angelo Mosca or hockey's Gordie Howe could have lasted more than a minute in the ring with Mean Gene.

He was also a great entertainer. He promised $10 of pleasure for every dollar spent on a ticket. He once initiated a riot in Toronto by tearing up a $1,000 cheque presented to Whipper Billy Watson, his frequent rival and a beloved fan favourite.

Kiniski was the youngest of six children born to a poor family in hardscrabble rural Alberta. His father worked as a $5-a-week barber, while his Polish-born mother sold cosmetics door to door and managed a café. When Gene was fifteen, she went back to school to complete her education, interrupted in Grade 7. She contested eleven elections before winning a seat on Edmonton city council, where she proved a formidable advocate for the poor. Every year, on her birthday, Gene made sure she received a bottle of Joy perfume.

Long after her death, her son said even the slightest rose-and-jasmine whiff of her favourite perfume reduced him to tears.

He spent three seasons with the Edmonton Eskimos, but he learned he could make more money in the ring. Incredibly, his first ring nickname was "Skinny Gene Kiniski."

Mean Gene settled in Vancouver in the early 1960s, touting the city's beauty at every opportunity. He was a proud Canadian, even after establishing his residence just across the border in Washington state. He owned the Reef Tavern in Point Roberts, a popular watering hole for thirsty Canadians, especially on Sunday in the days when British Columbia's liquor laws were still influenced by Prohibition.

Kiniski finally retired from the ring at age sixty-four because he said no one wanted to see an old guy beat the crap out of a young guy.

Wrestling World magazine once featured a full-colour photograph on its cover of Kiniski using a ring rope to choke into submission some hapless opponent. The headline read, "I'm Not Afraid Of Anything, by Gene Kiniski."

True, he was not afraid of any man, but Kiniski admitted to being intimidated by the movie camera.

He appeared in *Double Happiness* as Man at Bus Stop and as a wrestler in Sylvester Stallone's *Paradise Alley*. He portrayed a sadistic cop in *Terminal City Ricochet*.

"It was a humbling experience," he told me afterwards. "I was completely out of my element."

He did not think he had much of a future on the big screen.

"With my face, my voice and my features, maybe I can get a character role. My capabilities are limited. Even on a commercial, there's a goddamned cattle call. Who needs it?"

April 21, 2010

CHARACTERS

From Depression years until 1979, Foncie Pulice patrolled a stretch of sidewalk in downtown Vancouver, snapping photographs of passersby in hopes they might purchase his prints. He was a Karsh of the concrete. Here he propositions a potential customer in 1970. PHOTO BY DENI EAGLAND, PROVIDED BY THE *VANCOUVER SUN*

Foncie Pulice

STREET PHOTOGRAPHER

(MAY 8, 1914—JANUARY 20, 2003)

Foncie Pulice worked the bustling sidewalks of downtown Vancouver, taking casual snapshots of passersby, who could purchase prints the next day. He was known as the "Karsh of the Concrete."

He began hustling as a street photographer in 1934, and over the years leading to his retirement in 1979 became a fixture in the daily routine of workers and shoppers.

He took as his subject the passing parade: couples in their Saturday-night finery; families off to a matinee; soldiers and sailors on leave; bag-toting women on a shopping expedition; young toughs in aviator sunglasses and black leather jackets; fur-bedecked women holding lap dogs.

Each received a small card from Foncie's Fotos. "Call and see a natural living picture of yourself and friends for a lasting souvenir." The photos were three for fifty cents, six for seventy-five cents, or eight for a buck.

He was an indefatigable portraitist, his workday beginning as the first early-bird office workers stepped off the trolley bus, and ending when the last popcorn-sated habitués left the theatre.

Pulice compensated for a lack of artistry by injecting a vibrant spontaneity into all of his portraits. He patrolled the sidewalks of Granville, Robson and Hastings streets, becoming over the years an unofficial chronicler of trends in fashion, hairstyles and, as can be seen in his backgrounds, architecture.

He was known to up-and-comers and down-and-outers. "I had doctors, lawyers, you name it," he once told reporter John Mackie. "Celebrities. Van Johnson, the Mills Brothers." His lens was a democratic tool as he snapped poses of Natives, Chinese Canadians and Indo-Canadians, some of whom the law may have had yet to recognize as full citizens, but whose dollars were the same green to the photographer as that of any of his subjects.

After all, the wealthy could afford formal studio portraits. Everyone else paraded to Foncie's Fotos. "I used to get families down every year, they'd come down Granville to get their photo from Foncie," he said.

The amiable, pint-sized lensman pushed a jerry-rigged cart decorated by a sign advertising "Electric Photos" in red letters offset by a blue lightning bolt. A camera with a flash lamp and round reflector was mounted atop the strange contraption, which was powered by a car battery.

"It's like what your dad would have come up with by tinkering down in the basement," said Vancouver Museum history curator Joan Seidl. Pulice donated his cart to the museum, which has put it on display with a scrapbook of his photographs.

On retirement, the newspapers bid adieu to a golden age of sidewalk commerce, as Pulice was the last vestige of a time when newsboys hawked the late edition, and pedestrians sampled the aromatic wares of chip wagons. Only in recent years has his contribution to city life gained recognition. A newspaper item calling for donations of his photos attracted more than three hundred nostalgic residents to the museum.

His works were included in photographic shows in 1994 and 2001 at the Presentation House Gallery in North Vancouver. So ubiquitous was Pulice that among his photos was a street portrait of a rival street photographer.

Alfonso Agostino Pulice was born in Victoria to Italian parents who had emigrated from Calabria. His family moved to Vancouver when he was a boy, and he grew up in the hardscrabble Strathcona neighbourhood, where he got the lifelong nickname "Foncie."

Job opportunities for Italian Canadians were limited, so Pulice worked as a house painter until hired at age twenty to assist Joe Iaci, a street photographer. He was paid only forty cents for every one hundred photos, but he was able to shoot as many as fifteen hundred in a day.

After Canada went to war against Germany and Italy, Pulice enlisted in the Canadian Armed Forces. He was an opponent of fascism, his son Anthony Pulice said, who felt it important to take a stand against the government of his ancestral homeland. He spent his years in service based in Canada.

He hit the streets again in 1946 with his own business. Though his business competed against a handful of rivals, Foncie's Fotos would become a byword for street photography in Vancouver. He eventually bought out all competitors. Although his working day was usually spent on the street, Pulice operated a small storefront studio for passport and other commercial photography. The hundreds of daily images were developed overnight in the basement of the family home.

The punishing schedule was necessary because Pulice had to have a print available for his potential customers the day after they had been photographed. Perhaps not surprisingly, no one else in the family showed a subsequent passion for photography.

March 25, 2003

William Clancey wears a flamboyant white suit while walking alongside Premier W.A.C. Bennett in 1972. A shameless publicist and unapologetic partisan, Clancey put the razzle-dazzle in Social Credit's first two decades of power. PHOTO BY GEORGE DIACK, PROVIDED BY THE *VANCOUVER SUN*

WILLIAM CLANCEY

POLITICAL PUBLICIST

(APRIL 18, 1915—DECEMBER 5, 2004)

William (Bill) Clancey was a garrulous publicist who conjured razzle-dazzle for British Columbia's first Social Credit era.

Clancey became a friend and confidant of Premier W.A.C. Bennett, with whom he travelled the province while dreaming up outrageous stunts and flim-flammery. One author described him as Social Credit's "court jester."

The publicist was sidekick to the politician, organizing photo opportunities at the opening of dams and railroads where he would take a place at the right hand of his boss. He never ran for office himself, yet exercised an influence on the province for more than fifteen years.

Theirs was an unlikely political marriage. Bennett, a hardware merchant, was famously a teetotal Conservative and Mason. Clancey was a Liberal and a Roman Catholic who liked his liquor. A spirited game of gin rummy with Clancey was the closest Bennett ever came to alcohol.

This odd couple once travelled to Las Vegas. The premier was not led into temptation by the many delights on offer in Sin City, USA. "He didn't gamble," Clancey said. "Wouldn't even look at the girls!"

Clancey always addressed the premier as "Chief." Bennett in turn referred to his friend as "The Senator," a nickname that carried an inside joke as a promise to be fulfilled when Bennett became prime minister.

As it was, Bennett did not need a federal office to take for himself the title of Prime Minister of British Columbia, an honorific that graced his letterhead and with which he insisted on being called. Many assumed the pompous presumption of the title was Clancey's handiwork, a parentage he always denied.

His expertise was balloons and brass bands, straw hats and noise-makers. If Bennett was trailing in one of the province's hamburger polls, in which restaurant patrons ordered a sandwich named after a politician, Clancey would organize the purchase of Bennett Burgers by the bagful. He wished for his man to finish atop even a grease poll.

On at least one occasion when Clancey resorted to a dirty trick the tactic backfired. Pat McGeer, a neurosurgeon at the University of British Columbia, was the Liberal candidate in a 1962 by-election when he was the guest on a live open-line radio program. An unidentified caller asked, "Dr. McGeer, are you still putting needles in monkeys' heads out there at the university?"

Into the chasm of silence stepped Liberal Leader Ray Perrault, who was also in the studio. He told the audience that he recognized the unmistakable folksy intonation of the caller and introduced him to the listening audience as the premier's right-hand man.

Many years later, Clancey confirmed the story to columnist Vaughn Palmer, adding the delicious detail that he had made the call in Bennett's presence, though the premier urged him not to do so because he might be caught out.

"Bill Clancey was an outrageous kind of circus master, the man who organized bond-burnings and drum-beatings and ensured that Bennett never experienced what the poet Robert Frost called the hell of a half-filled auditorium," historian David J. Mitchell noted in *W.A.C.*, his 1983 biography.

"Initially, Bennett was attracted to Clancey simply because he was so very unlike anyone he had previously met. Clancey was good at getting the crowds out, the bands playing, loud speakers blaring and all the old-time political hype that Bennett thrived on."

William Edward Stephen Clancey was born in Calgary, moving with his family to Vancouver as a baby. He became president of the Young Liberal Association and found employment under the patronage of Prime Minister William Lyon Mackenzie King. He then worked for Duff Pattullo, the Liberal premier of BC.

The Liberals formed a wartime coalition with the Conservatives in which Mr. Bennett was a freshly elected MLA. The parties formed a bloc to limit the electoral success of the socialist Co-operative Commonwealth Federation, the forerunner to today's NDP.

The coalition collapsed prior to the 1952 election, from which the renegade Bennett arose with an unknown coterie of MLAs. When he managed to form a minority government, Clancey found himself for the first time not aligned with the party in power.

The following year he opened William Clancey and Associates, a public-relations firm. He remained a Liberal and a critic of the ragtag Socreds.

He became a convert only after meeting Bennett while organizing ceremonies for the opening of the Oak Street Bridge connecting Vancouver to suburban Richmond. A friendship sown at a ribbon-cutting would flourish at many similar events.

Clancey's account of their first formal conversation in the premier's office at the Legislature in Victoria was included in a book published in 1990.

"Mr. Clancey, I take for granted that you have been in this office before," Bennett said.

"I also know you are a good Catholic.

"I know you take a drink.

"I know you are Liberal."

Clancey replied: "I know you are a good Mason.

"I know you do not take a drink.

"I know you are an ex-Conservative."

Clancey's most memorable stunt was the burning of government bonds in 1959. On a beautiful summer's evening in Kelowna, about ten thousand people gathered on the shores of Okanagan Lake, where a raft had been loaded with $70-million in bonds. The notes were surrounded by wood shavings and old car tires, all doused in oil.

Bennett, joined by two cabinet ministers and the omnipresent Clancey, rode a boat out into the lake. At 9:27 p.m. on August 1, seven years to the minute of his swearing-in as premier, Bennett fired an arrow onto the raft, which soon was ablaze to the cheers of the crowd.

The brilliant publicity coup was also a typical bit of Socred legerdemain. The premier's arrow had bounced off the raft and fizzled in the lake. A Mountie had been placed on the barge with a torch, which he dutifully used to turn the bonds into ash.

Another time, a mix-up led to the premier being directly invited to meet with US President John F. Kennedy in Seattle. (The invitation should have been extended through the federal government. Perhaps the American protocol officers had been bamboozled by the premier's grandiloquent claim to a prime ministerial title.) A bourbon-sipping Clancey took the opportunity to expound on Social Credit's philosophy for the benefit of the president.

Bennett retired from politics soon after the Socreds were defeated in the 1972 election. The hiatus from power would last but three years for the Socreds, yet Clancey never again achieved such public prominence as he had during his friendship with the premier.

Clancey remained busy with his firm and held executive positions with energy, banking and mining companies. He chased gold claims in Nevada and was front man for a grand scheme to slake California's thirst by diverting a British Columbia river.

The proposed $3.8-billion development involved damming the North Thompson River, a tributary of the Fraser; diverting water to Canoe Reach in the Columbia River watershed; allowing water to flow southward to the John Day Dam on the Oregon–Washington border; and building a pipeline that would transport water across five hundred kilometres of the Oregon plateau to a lake near Alturas, California, where it could then flow to the Shasta Reservoir. The diversion would make one million acre-feet of water available to the Los Angeles basin. The water was to be sold at $1,000 per acre.

Environmentalists complained about the project, which did not survive several temporary government moratoriums on bulk shipments of water.

Clancey could not fathom the objections.

"It is not water that we would take from anywhere," he said. "It's water that was going to the sea."

Clancey was a founding director of the Bank of British Columbia, a convocation founder of Simon Fraser University, and an original director of the BC Lions football team, which ensconced him on the club's Wall of Fame at BC Place Stadium in 2002. He was an organizer of the 1958 provincial centennial celebrations, as well as the originator and commissioner of the BC Year of Music in 1991.

Late in life, he became a British Columbia separatist, writing a book extolling the benefits of an independent nation. Clancey called for a referendum before the declaration of an independent British Columbia, which would become a neutral nation like Switzerland.

His self-published manifesto was titled *The New Dominion of British Columbia*. The book warned of a "dictatorship of minorities" and blamed uncontrolled immigration for a rise in "Oriental youth gangs." Clancey also opposed bilingualism, the metric system and the settling of aboriginal land claims.

The book failed to ignite interest other than as a curiosity in a province with no shortage of political oddballs.

February 27, 2004

Sheldon Luck (right) stands on a dock in Kitimat in 1952 with the postmaster, who holds the first ever consignment of airmail flown from Vancouver. He was a bush pilot who lived up to his name by surviving many close calls. PHOTO COURTESY OF CANADA'S AVIATION HALL OF FAME

Sheldon Luck

BUSH PILOT

(JANUARY 26, 1911—MAY 9, 2004)

Sheldon Luck was one of those fearless bush pilots whose exploits could have been scripted by Hollywood. He flew mercy missions in miserable weather, delivered miners to isolated claims (and prostitutes to boom towns), and piloted Robert Service on the Sourdough poet's first flight over the Yukon he immortalized.

Luck spent the early years of a five-decade career flying underpowered aircraft in unspeakable conditions to locations so remote as to have been unnamed and unmapped. After walking away from several wrecks, Luck was described as a pilot who lived up to his family name. His adventures were chronicled by the *New York Times* and the *Saturday Evening Post*. Gordon Sinclair wrote in the *Toronto Daily Star* that the pilot's "charmed life is the talk of the north."

His many accomplishments included the first airmail delivery between Vancouver and Whitehorse. He is credited with making a nighttime crossing of the Rocky Mountains by the light of lit matchsticks. He also inaugurated scheduled commercial service to several cities in the British Columbia Interior, including Kamloops and Prince George.

During the Second World War, he dodged German fighters

by hiding in clouds off the coast of occupied France. He also received a king's commendation for ferrying top-secret messages and other mail while Winston Churchill was attending the Quebec Conference in 1943.

His most harrowing incident took place over Newfoundland during the war, when smoke in the cabin panicked his passengers, four of whom jumped from the plane—two without parachutes.

Nor was he ever far removed from the reminders of danger. In 1935, he crossed paths on the ground with a plane returning with the bodies of Wiley Post and Will Rogers after their death in a crash in Alaska, a reminder of man's hubris in wishing to fly.

Standing six foot one with a broad nose and a thin Errol Flynn moustache, Luck presented a dashing figure at all times, whether as a young man wrapped in furs and stuffed into a cramped open cockpit, or as a respected aviator wearing a crisp uniform and handling streamlined aircraft as chief pilot for Canadian Pacific Air Lines. He was, in the words of one biographer, a "smooth-talking, easy-walking, professional pilot."

William Floyd Sheldon Luck was born in Kingston, Ontario, the third of four children of Minnie and Rev. H.B. Luck, a Free Methodist minister who had in mind for his son loftier pursuits than joyriding in an airplane. Moving west with his family, young Sheldon became obsessed with flight as a boy watching such Great War veterans as Wop May flying at the Edmonton airstrip. He enrolled at the Rutledge Air Services flying school after the family settled in Calgary, earning money for tuition by hauling manure from the stockyards at fifty cents an hour. At night, he moonlighted as a house detective at the Grand Theatre.

Luck's first solo flight came on Christmas Eve 1930. "Suddenly, I was airborne," he told Ted Beaudoin for the biography *Walking on Air*. "I was a birdman, flying, and there was nobody else in the cockpit in front of me. I really was on my own." He was just nineteen.

To earn a commercial licence, Luck needed to rent an airplane to accumulate hours of flying time, an expense far beyond his means during those Depression days. His pilot's licence allowed him to carry passengers, but not to charge a fee. The solution was practical, if not entirely legal, he once told aviation historian Peter Corley-Smith.

"I'd say to the passenger: 'Do you want to go for a ride?' and I'd explain it to him. So he'd give me the money and we'd go . . . back to the clubhouse and pay for the rental of the machine, and that way you build up hours, and sometimes you'd be lucky and get in two or three hours over the weekend."

The commercial licence he earned was No. 102.

In 1935, he acquired a de Havilland Puss Moth, forming Advanced Air Services in Calgary with a wealthy widow and her son, a business venture that was as unlikely as it was short-lived. In those days, pilots had few of the navigational tools now available, relying instead on radio as well as experience, anecdote and intuition.

Later that year, after completing a charter flight to Williams Lake, a homesick Luck decided to risk a nighttime return. The perilous crossing was made worse when a dead battery extinguished panel lights inside the small aircraft. Ron Campbell, a mechanic, had to strike matches to allow Luck a glance at instruments. A break in the clouds and the chance sighting of the lights of the Ghost dam eased the return home of a flight that entered the record books as the first west-to-east, night crossing of the Rockies.

He found work flying whitefish from remote Alberta lakes destined for Chicago restaurant tables. On March 6, 1936, with a full load of fish in the hold, his Boeing crashed shortly after takeoff as Luck tried to return for an emergency landing on Peerless Lake. Instead, he clipped trees. The engine tore through the plane, reducing the load to a mess of fish guts and oil. Luck was pulled from the wreckage, which then burned. He had lost not only his load but his sole source of income.

He was soon hired as a pilot by Grant McConachie, a fish-hauling rival said to have been impressed by Luck's skill in crash-landing the Boeing. Luck spent six years with United Air Transport, which was re-organized as Yukon Southern Air Transport before joining other companies as part of Canadian Pacific Air Lines.

Luck inaugurated a Vancouver–Whitehorse airmail and passenger run aboard a Norseman seaplane. He also opened postal delivery by air to hamlets such as Gold Bar (since flooded by the waters of Williston Reservoir), as well as to Zeballos, a gold-mining town on Vancouver Island.

Luck was carrying a load of gold, as well as three passengers and a dog, when his Fleet suddenly lost power outside Lower Post, near the British Columbia–Yukon border. With fog rising from the Liard River, making a water landing impossible, he chose a canopy of second-growth trees in which to settle his machine in a risky manoeuvre known as "walking the tree tops." After the craft came to a jarring halt, Luck discovered the only casualty was the dog.

In 1942, he volunteered as a civilian pilot with the Royal Air Force's Ferry Command, flying B-17s, B-24 Liberators and B-26 Marauders across the Atlantic to England and Africa.

In May 1943, he was transporting eighteen service personnel to Gander, Newfoundland, when smoke in the cockpit and cabin panicked some of the passengers. According to *Walking on Air*, four men jumped from the Ventura in the chaos. The two who wore parachutes were found by accident fifty days later, exhausted and starving. The bodies of the others were never recovered.

Luck returned to Canadian Pacific after the war, soon leaving for the promise of a doubled salary as chief instructor with FAMA (Flota Aerea Mercante Argentina) in Buenos Aires. However, political uncertainty after Juan Peron regained power soon had him back in British Columbia.

He bounced around several regional airlines, including a stint with Queen Charlotte Airlines, Jim Spilsbury's so-called "accidental airline." He also farmed and ranched, although he maintained his pilot's licence for fifty-four years until deciding not to renew it at age seventy-three. He spent many of his later years piloting water bombers over forest fires. He also learned to fly jet planes after turning sixty. In all, he was said to have mastered fifty-nine different types of airplane.

Luck knew anyone who was anybody in the early days of aviation in the North. He counted among his friends not only such visionaries as Grant McConachie but Pacific Western Airlines founder Russ Baker and Wardair founder Max Ward, with whom he once shared digs. While the trio all earned fame and fortune as managers and entrepreneurs, Luck resisted their entreaties to abandon the cockpit for the boardroom.

He was inducted into the Canadian Aviation Hall of Fame in 1981, the same year he became a companion of the Order of Icarus, which honours those Canadians whose airborne skills advanced manned flight.

In 1982, Luck was a mystery guest on CBC-TV's *Front Page Challenge*. The panelists were stumped in trying to guess his identity. Among them was Gordon Sinclair, who had interviewed him forty-one years earlier.

Luck died of lung cancer at a hospice in Kamloops. He did not want a funeral service. He asked for his ashes to be scattered by the wind at Fort St. James.

An unofficial memorial and a testament to his skill exists not far from the south bank of the Liard River outside Lower Post near the Yukon border, where rests the wreckage of the Fleet crashed so many years ago. To this day, a float from the plane can be spotted overhead in a tree branch.

May 24, 2004

Acknowledgements

Bruce Smillie worked as the night city editor of the *Vancouver Sun* for many years. Mr. Nightside, as he was known, had advice for young reporters looking for a story on a slow news day. "Check the obits," he'd say. "Always a story in there."

Smillie was correct. The paid obituary notices published in a newspaper's classified section are a gold mine. Some of the characters in this book were first spotted in the small print of a newspaper and I thank my friends and readers for bringing those to my attention.

Most of these stories were originally published in slightly different form in the *Globe and Mail*. Thanks to editors Colin Haskin, David Walmsley, Susan Smith and the *Globe*'s crew of copyeditors who saved me from myself more than once.

A die-hard band of online obit fans at alt.obituaries track the work of those of us on the "dead beat." I much appreciate the encouraging words I've had from Bill Schenley and Amelia Rosner.

Kit Krieger conjured the title for this book during a brainstorming session with John Mackie, Don Prior and Carlyn Yandle. (Among the also-rans: "*B.C. R.I.P.*") Kit's younger brother, Bob, a cartoonist for the *Province*, offered more laughs and hospitality than any writer deserves.

The author photograph used in promotional materials was shot by the talented Deddeda White. Tom Barrett came up with the funny line about being an "award-losing journalist." Patricia Wolfe gave the manuscript a welcomed polish. Thanks to the publisher and smart crew at Harbour—Anna Comfort O'Keeffe, Marisa Alps, Teresa Karbashewski, Mary White, Elaine Park and Tyler Laing, who did yeoman work in tracking down photographs.

My mother, Joyce, instilled in me an early love for reading. My late father, a high-school teacher whose name I carry, told me stories about some of the people in this book before his own death in 2002. My children, John and Nellie, and their mother, Debbie Wilson, surrendered the dining-room table for the duration without complaint.

Please let me know of any errors at tomhawthorn@gmail.com. Don't be shy. After all, the subjects are in no condition to complain.